Artificial Intelligence – A Primer for State and Local Government

Everything you need to know since yesterday

Alan R. Shark

(with ChatGPT, Google Gemini, Perplexity AI, DALL-E)

About the cover

The cover art was appropriately AI-generated. The author's prompt was simply to "draw a picture of an octopus, sitting atop masses of data, both structured and unstructured – including social media." So why an Octopus? The Octopus was chosen to try to make the (abstract) point that data underlies all of AI. The Octopus has eight legs and hundreds to thousands of suckers, depending on size and species, that help it navigate, protect itself from perceived dangers, and select, manipulate, and digest food. The Octopus is also highly curious, intelligent, and surprisingly good at problem-solving; they possess a great deal of memory and can change their appearance to blend into their environment. Its unique shape allows the Octopus to sense and touch everything from every direction.

About the Illustrations

Each cartoon illustration was generated from author prompts and OpenAI's image program, DALL-E.

Acknowledgments

As the title page suggests, generative AI played an essential role in compiling this book, which was edited by AI-powered Grammarly.

CONTENTS

PREFACE

Welcome to "A Primer on AI for State and Local Government," where knowledge meets innovation, and possibilities abound.

The government landscape is undergoing a significant transformation driven by the power of artificial intelligence (AI). From streamlining administrative tasks to informing data-driven policy decisions, AI offers many opportunities to enhance efficiency, improve constituent services, and optimize resource allocation at the state and local levels.

This primer was designed to serve as a comprehensive guide for state and local government officials, employees, and policymakers seeking to understand and leverage AI's potential. We delve into the core concepts of AI technology, exploring its various applications within the government sector. Practical examples highlight how AI is already utilized to address real-world challenges municipalities and state agencies face.

We recognize that alongside AI's immense potential lie critical considerations. This primer addresses the ethical implications and potential biases inherent in AI systems. We explore strategies for responsible AI implementation, ensuring transparency, fairness, and accountability in government operations.

Whether you are a policymaker crafting legislation, a public administrator overseeing service delivery, or a technologist implementing AI solutions, this primer equips you with the knowledge and tools needed to make informed decisions and drive positive outcomes for your community.

Ultimately, this primer equips state and local governments with the knowledge and tools necessary to navigate the evolving world of AI. By fostering a comprehensive understanding of this powerful technology, governments can harness its potential to build a more efficient, responsive, and citizen-centric future. This book is formatted with easy-to-digest content delivered in outline style.

The subtitle, "Everything you need to know since yesterday," is the author's way of saying that AI is changing almost every day with new applications, opportunities, and new challenges. This book was written with care to make sure the very latest was incorporated before publication – so it is best to view this book as foundational with the understanding it is only a guide or starting point for public managers.

A Poem on AI for Cities and Counties

In cities and counties, where progress takes flight, AI lends a hand, with its digital might. It weaves through the streets like a silent guide, Improving our lives on this technological ride.

In urban landscapes, where challenges abound, AI steps in, to turn things around. Traffic congestion is a perennial woe. With smart algorithms, it finds the best flow.

For public safety, it's a guardian true, Predicting crime patterns before they ensue. AI watches over us with eyes that endure surveillance with the purpose of keeping us secure.

In government offices, where paperwork thrives, AI streamlines tasks, and efficiency thrives. Bureaucracy's red tape helps to untangle, Making services swift for all who wrangle.

In healthcare and education, it plays a part in diagnosing diseases with a compassionate heart. Customized learning for diverse students, AI adapts and nurtures them as they traverse.

It tackles environmental concerns with grace, Optimizing resources in the right place. From energy usage to waste reduction, AI aids in sustainability, a vital deduction.

In cities and counties, AI takes the lead, Solving problems with insight and speed. But let us remember, as we stride on this trail, To keep ethics in mind, and justice prevail.

For AI, though a tool, must serve all, not few. The future it shapes is up to me and you. With wisdom and foresight, we'll pave the way To

In cities and counties, AI takes the lead, Solving problems with insight and speed. But let us remember, as we stride on this trail, To keep ethics in mind, and justice prevail.

For AI, though a tool, must serve all, not few. The future it shapes is up to me and you. With wisdom and foresight, we'll pave the way To build cities and counties where all can thrive each day.

Prompted by Alan R. Shark
Created by ChatGPT

CHAPTER ONE
An Introduction To Artificial Intelligence

AI, or Artificial Intelligence, refers to the simulation of human intelligence processes by machines, particularly computer systems. This includes learning, reasoning, problem-solving, perception, and decision-making capabilities to emulate human-like behavior and cognition. The talk of AI was always in the background until early 2022 with the introduction of OpenAI's ChatGPT. This was when the public began to notice and learn about the power, potential, and pitfalls of generative AI. As with most forms of innovative technology, related laws, regulations, and policies always lag far behind. But that hasn't stopped state and local governments from experimenting and developing innovative applications. Today AI appears to be everywhere. With every household appliance and every new laptop, all are claiming to be AI-infused - it makes one wonder what exactly AI is and whether all these claims are justified.

The talk of artificial intelligence (AI) dates back to antiquity, with myths and rumors of artificially intelligent beings from other worlds. However, the modern concept of AI began to take shape in the early 20th century, with the groundwork laid in the 1900s and where major strides were made in the 1950s. Significant developments include the creation of the first artificial neural network, the development of the Perceptron, and the introduction of the Turing test. The 1980s showed a period of rapid growth and interest in AI, known as the "AI boom," marked by breakthroughs in research and increased government funding. Today, AI has become a pervasive force, impacting various aspects of our lives, from healthcare to business. The field has seen exponential growth in training computation, leading to more powerful AI systems. The history of AI provides an important context for understanding its current state and potential future developments.

Artificial Intelligence (AI) refers to the simulation of human intelligence in machines that are programmed to think like humans and mimic their actions. This can include learning, reasoning, problem-solving, perception, and language understanding. AI systems can range from simple applications like a recommendation algorithm in a shopping app to complex autonomous robots. Central to AI is the ability to process substantial amounts of data and learn from it, allowing the system to adapt and improve its performance over time. AI technologies are increasingly integrated into various sectors, revolutionizing industries by providing enhanced data analytics, automation, and novel solutions to complex problems.

Many, like this author, believe that AI as deployed today is more akin to Augmented Intelligence which can be defined as:

> *"…. the theory and development of computer systems able to supplement human decision making, planning, and forecasting based on abundant sources of quality data."*

So much of what fascinates us today is the use of the large language model. A large language model (LLM) is an artificial intelligence program that processes, understands, and generates human language based on immense text datasets. These models, such as GPT (Generative Pre-trained Transformer), are trained using deep learning techniques, specifically neural networks, on vast amounts of textual data. During this training process, they learn language patterns, grammar, nuances, and even the context in which words and phrases are used.

The "large" in their name refers to both the size of the training data and the complexity of the neural networks involved. These models have millions, or even billions, of parameters, which are the parts of the model that are learned from training data. After training, an LLM can perform a wide range of language-related tasks. These include but are not limited to writing essays, summarizing text, translating languages, answering questions, and even creating content like poems or computer code.

What sets these models apart is their ability to generate coherent and contextually relevant text over extended passages, understand and respond to queries, and even engage in conversations that feel natural. This capability stems from their understanding of language patterns and nuances learned during training. However, it's important to note that while LLMs are powerful tools, they are not without limitations and do not possess true understanding or consciousness. They are tools that mimic language understanding based on patterns in the data on which they have been trained.

Another term often discussed is Machine Learning, which begs the question, what is the difference between machine learning and AI? Artificial intelligence (AI) is the broader concept of enabling a machine or system to sense, reason, act, or adapt like a human. On the other hand, machine learning (ML) is an application of AI that allows machines to extract knowledge from data and learn from it. In simpler terms, AI is the general ability of computers to emulate human thought, while ML is a specific method for achieving AI. AI encompasses a wide variety of specific approaches, while ML is just one of the subfields under the AI umbrella, along with other subfields such as deep learning, robotics, expert systems, and natural language processing.

Some have compared the popularity to another over-hyped technology like Cloud computing or blockchain technologies that overpromise, are overhyped, and soon either disappear or slowly take hold with little fanfare. According to Statista, it took Netflix 3.5 years to reach 1 million users in 2009 and ChatGPT achieved 1 million users in just 5 days in 2022.

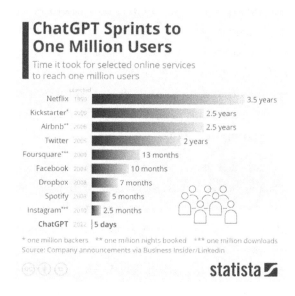

From this author's personal experience with AI in general and generative AI specifically, this is the most significant advancement in technology since the Internet became available to the public. State and local governments are often viewed as the front lines of innovation.

Hopefully, this book will provide a solid foundation for understanding AI and its potential for positive innovation as well as the challenges of misuse or even worse.

The big question everyone asks is where the applications are. Many see policies and guidelines, but few see outward examples of their deployment. Adoption has been as subtle as it is pervasive. Nearly all current AI applications occur at the individual level. Microsoft has added AI to its ever-popular Office 365 with its Co-Pilot feature that empowers its users to be ever more productive and creative in using its suite of products, like Word, PowerPoint, and Excel applications. Those who work with data of almost any kind can utilize AI to seek clues, patterns, and anomalies and generate leads, reports, summations, and graphic illustrations.

The Art of the Prompt

Knowing how to ask a question is paramount in obtaining the desired results regarding AI. This is referred to as a prompt. Sometimes the simple rewording or rephrasing of a prompt can yield differing results or disappointment. The prompt is crucial when it comes to interacting with AI models as it serves as the input or guidance for generating responses. The quality, specificity, and clarity of the prompt significantly influence the relevance and accuracy of the AI's output. A well-crafted prompt can guide the AI to produce more relevant and useful responses, while a vague or ambiguous prompt may result in less coherent or accurate outputs. Therefore, understanding how to formulate effective prompts is essential for maximizing the utility of AI systems in various applications. Further, we must realize that AI doesn't really possess human intelligence (at least not yet) as it focuses on providing what it perceives as the desired outcome. Generative AI systems are focused on compiling an educated guess based on their training instead of verifying facts and authenticity.

Knowing this basic AI characteristic demands careful attention to any AI output. We humans cannot pass off AI outputs without taking responsibility for their accuracy, bias, ethics, and even attributions.

State and local government workers will require training in the "art of the prompt" since the clearer the prompt the better the odds of obtaining a desired result. This could lead to greater productivity and more accurate informed data for enhanced decision-making.

What (Else) Can Go Wrong?

Despite the amazing things AI can perform in all its forms, there are serious problems that require understanding and action. Among the most serious are providing what appears to be factual information but is actually absolutely false, called hallucinations. Then there are the issues of bias and ethics. After all, it stands to reason that since so much of generative AI is trained on human documentation, it is only natural for AI systems to learn from "us," inheriting our conscious and unconscious biases and ethical challenges.

Ethics and Bias

Issues of ethics and bias in AI are incredibly serious and have profound implications for individuals and society. Areas of common concern are:

- Impact on Individuals and Society: Biases in AI systems can perpetuate and amplify societal inequalities, leading to discriminatory outcomes in areas such as hiring, lending, criminal justice, and healthcare. These biases can result in unfair treatment, marginalization, and exacerbation of existing social disparities.

- Trust and Acceptance: Ethical concerns surrounding AI, including issues of bias, transparency, accountability, and privacy, can erode trust in AI technologies. Lack of trust may hinder the adoption and acceptance of AI systems, limiting their potential benefits to society.

- Legal and Regulatory Implications: As AI technologies become more pervasive, there's a growing need for regulations and legal frameworks to address ethical considerations and mitigate potential harm. Failure to address ethical issues in AI could lead to legal challenges, regulatory fines, and reputational damage for organizations deploying AI systems.

- Human Rights and Dignity: Ethical AI development should prioritize protecting human rights and dignity. Biased AI systems can potentially infringe upon individuals' rights to fairness, non-discrimination, privacy, and autonomy.

- Long-Term Implication: The decisions made by AI systems can have long-lasting and far-reaching consequences. Ethical considerations must be integrated into the entire lifecycle of AI development, from data collection and model training to deployment and impact assessment, to ensure that AI technologies serve the greater good and align with societal values.

While bias is considered one of the leading concerns of AI, we rarely hear about another term that can be as significant – it is "prejudice". Some believe they are one and the same, but bias and prejudice in AI are closely related, yet they have distinct nuances. Bias refers to the inherent slant or unfairness in the data used to train an AI system. This can arise from various factors like:

- Addressing issues of ethics, bias, and prejudice in AI requires a multi-stakeholder approach involving collaboration between policymakers, technologists, ethicists, researchers, civil society organizations, and the public. It involves implementing measures such as diversity in dataset collection, transparent and accountable AI algorithms, ethical guidelines and standards, bias detection and mitigation techniques, and ongoing monitoring and evaluation of AI systems' impacts on society.

- By prioritizing ethics and bias mitigation in AI development, we can strive to create more equitable, trustworthy, and beneficial AI technologies for all.

Caution Ahead

Today, AI starts with us. Generative AI can provide great-looking – but false information. You should try it and experiment, knowing that, ultimately, you are responsible for anything you may use. It can be useful in creating outlines, summaries, information, and data. It can generate poems, images, and illustrations, but early AI systems have been known to generate bias and violate ethical norms. Government managers must be very watchful of any AI used for citizen communications, deepfake videos and audio presentations, and misinformation that is aimed at influencing elections or causing further erosion of trust or pitting citizens against one another. Worse, there are many nation-state actors who are perpetuating disinformation, masquerading as normal-looking citizens who, in reality, do not exist.

As we know, AI appears to be everywhere, and questions remain as to what it can do in all of its many forms. AI, as we understand it today, can mean Automated Intelligence, Augmented Intelligence, and Artificial Intelligence. While this primer covers AI generally, it will focus on generative AI more specifically, and there are many new entrants to this growing field.

- Selection bias occurs when the training data does not represent the real world and is skewed toward a certain group.

- Data bias: When the data reflects existing societal prejudices like criminal records disproportionately affecting certain demographics.

Prejudice is a stronger term implying a preconceived negative attitude towards a particular group. AI doesn't inherently hold prejudices, but biased training data can lead it to make discriminatory decisions that reflect those prejudices. Both bias and prejudice in AI can lead to unfair outcomes, highlighting the importance of using diverse and unbiased datasets to train AI systems.

Addressing issues of ethics, bias, and prejudice in AI requires a multi-stakeholder approach that involves collaboration between policymakers, technologists, ethicists, researchers, civil society organizations, and the public. It involves implementing measures such as diversity in dataset collection, transparent and accountable AI algorithms, ethical guidelines and standards, bias detection and mitigation techniques, and ongoing monitoring and evaluation of AI systems' impacts on society. By prioritizing ethics and bias mitigation in AI development, we can strive to create more equitable, trustworthy, and beneficial AI technologies for all.

Caution Ahead

Today, AI starts with us. Generative AI can provide great-looking – but false information. You should try it and experiment, knowing that, ultimately, you are responsible for anything you may use. It can be useful in creating outlines, summaries, information, and data. It can generate poems, images, and illustrations, but early AI systems have been known to generate bias and violate ethical norms. Government managers must be very watchful of any AI used for citizen communications, deepfake videos and audio presentations, and misinformation aimed at influencing elections or causing further erosion of trust or pitting citizens against one another. Worse, many nation-state actors are perpetuating disinformation, masquerading as normal-looking citizens who, in reality, do not exist.

AI appears to be everywhere, and questions remain as to what it can do in all of its many forms. AI, as we understand it today, can mean Automated Intelligence, Augmented Intelligence, and Artificial Intelligence. While this primer covers AI generally, it will focus on generative AI more specifically, and there are many new entrants to this growing field.

In the following chapters, we will delve deeper and explore how we can best use and approach AI for ourselves and our public organizations. There is much to learn about AI, and what it can do for us. At the very least, we can say that the art of search that we have been accustomed to for the past twenty years through our search (legacy) engines has changed forever. The possibilities are endless. When it comes to AI, it never hurts to ask – but be prepared for the answers you may be surprised – and that can be either good or bad- or both.

CHAPTER 2
Contemporary Issues In AI – A Deeper Dive

It wasn't until the end of 2022 that ChatGPT entered the public domain that we all had to learn what generative AI was all about. Its overnight success was something no less amazing as it took just five days to reach a million users. ChatGPT version 3.5 was trained on 175 billion parameters, and ChatGPT version 4 was trained on roughly 10 trillion words. No matter how one looks at such incomprehensible numbers - that's a lot of information we humans have produced. We continue learning about generative AI's power, potential, and pitfalls.

Today AI appears to be everywhere. With every household appliance featuring and every new laptop claiming to be AI-infused, one wonders what exactly AI is and whether all these claims are justified.

Countless professionals are already using AI to augment their work. They are creating outlines, summarizing data, writing code, summarizing action steps at meetings, writing memos, and even helping to draft articles. So, the AI we see today is from AI-assisted programs that remain mostly invisible except for its output, which often does not require attribution. By contrast, this book relies heavily on numerous AI platforms and AI-focused applications. Much of what we use today is really in the form of AI as *Augmented Intelligence* not so much *Artificial Intelligence.*

We are seeing AI manifest itself through human-like chatbots, deepfake photos and videos, and attractive AI-generated art. AI has changed the way we see (and hear) things where seeing is no longer believing. State and local governments have much in common regarding navigating AI applications within their jurisdictions.

To help better understand Artificial intelligence it has grown as a result of advancements in the following 6 areas.

1. Advancements in complex algorithms.

Advancements in AI algorithms have not only made AI systems more powerful and accurate but also more versatile and efficient, enabling their application in a myriad of industries and domains. Advancements in algorithms have significantly boosted the power of Artificial Intelligence (AI) in several ways:

- Improved Learning Efficiency: New algorithms have enhanced the learning efficiency of AI systems. They require less data to learn or can extract more information from existing data sets. This means AI can achieve higher accuracy with fewer resources.

- Deep Learning and Neural Networks: Developing deep learning algorithms that utilize layered neural networks has been a momentous change. These algorithms can process and interpret vast amounts of unstructured data, such as images, speech, or text, much more effectively than previous techniques.

- Increased Processing Power: Modern algorithms are designed to take full advantage of increased computing power, particularly with the advent of GPUs (Graphics Processing Units) and TPUs (Tensor Processing Units). These specialized processors can handle complex mathematical computations at a much faster rate, which is essential for training large AI models.

- Enhanced Decision Making: Advances in machine learning algorithms, especially in reinforcement learning, have enabled AI systems to make decisions and learn from the environment in a way that mimics human decision-making processes. This has led to breakthroughs in fields like robotics and autonomous vehicles.

- Scalability and Flexibility: New algorithms have facilitated the development of more scalable and flexible AI systems. They can be applied to a wider range of tasks and more easily adapted to unfamiliar problems or data sets.

- Optimization Techniques: Modern AI algorithms incorporate sophisticated optimization techniques, allowing them to find solutions to complex problems more efficiently. This is particularly important in logistics, resource allocation, and route planning.

- Reduced Bias and Improved Fairness: There is growing emphasis on designing algorithms that reduce bias and ensure fairness in AI decisions. This is crucial in applications like hiring, loan approvals, and law enforcement.

- Real-time Processing and Edge AI: Algorithm advancements have enabled real-time data processing and the emergence of edge AI, where AI computations are done on local devices rather than centralized servers. This reduces latency and allows for faster responses.

2. Dramatic Increase in speed and computing power.

Advancements in speed and computing power have been instrumental in overcoming AI's previous limitations, developing more complex, efficient, and effective AI systems, and opening up new possibilities across various fields.

- Handling Large Datasets: Modern AI, especially deep learning, requires processing vast amounts of data. Increased computing power allows for the more efficient handling and analysis of these big datasets, making it feasible to train more complex models.

- Improved Model Complexity: With greater computing power, AI models, particularly neural networks, can have more layers and parameters. This complexity enables them to capture subtler patterns and nuances in the data, leading to higher accuracy and more sophisticated AI capabilities.

- Faster Training Times: Enhanced speed reduces the time required to train AI models. What used to take weeks or months can now be accomplished in days or even hours. This acceleration allows for more iterative and experimental approaches in AI development.

- Enabling Real-time Processing: High-speed computing enables real-time data processing, which is critical in applications like autonomous vehicles, where immediate response to sensory input is essential. This real-time processing capability extends to other areas like healthcare diagnostics, financial trading, and smart devices.

- Scaling AI Applications: Increased computing power allows for the scaling of AI applications to handle more users, more complex tasks, and larger datasets without a loss in performance.

- Energy Efficiency: Advances in computing technology have focused on energy efficiency and raw power. This is vital for sustainable growth in AI, as training large models can be energy-intensive.

- Accessible AI: Improved computing power at lower costs has democratized access to AI technologies, enabling startups and smaller organizations to participate in AI development and innovation.

- Cloud Computing and Distributed Systems: The growth of cloud computing and distributed systems allows for harnessing computing power from multiple sources and locations. This has made managing and processing large-scale AI tasks easier without investing in expensive infrastructure.

3. Ability to digest data from various sources.

The ability of Artificial Intelligence (AI) to digest data from various sources results from several key developments in technology and methodology.

- Data Integration Techniques: AI systems have become adept at integrating data from multiple sources through advanced data integration techniques. These techniques include data normalization (making data from diverse sources compatible), data transformation, and using APIs (Application

Programming Interfaces) to aggregate and process data from different systems seamlessly.

- Advancements in Natural Language Processing (NLP): AI has made significant strides in understanding human language through NLP. This allows AI to extract and interpret data from text-based sources like websites, books, research papers, social media, and even unstructured data like emails and notes.

- Improvements in Image and Video Analysis: AI's ability to process and interpret visual data has grown immensely due to advancements in computer vision. This enables AI systems to extract information from images, videos, and live camera feeds, adding a rich layer of data that was previously difficult to utilize.

- Sensor Data Interpretation: The proliferation of IoT (Internet of Things) devices has led to an explosion in sensor-generated data. AI algorithms have become better at interpreting this data, ranging from temperature readings to complex industrial machine data.

- Scalable Storage and Cloud Computing: The advent of cloud computing and scalable storage solutions has allowed AI to access and process vast amounts of data from various sources without the limitations of local hardware constraints.

- Enhanced Machine Learning Algorithms: Machine learning algorithms have evolved to handle large and diverse datasets more effectively. Techniques like transfer learning allow AI systems to apply knowledge gained from one domain to another, enhancing their ability to digest varied data.

- Data Fusion and Multimodal Learning: AI systems are increasingly capable of data fusion, combining data from dissimilar sources and formats (like text, images, and sensor data) to create a more comprehensive understanding. Multimodal learning models are designed to process and interpret this mixed data.

- Robust Preprocessing Tools: Effective preprocessing tools and algorithms help clean, sort, and prepare data from diverse sources, making it suitable for AI analysis. This includes handling missing data, noise reduction, and feature extraction.

- Ethical and Privacy Considerations: With the ability to access diverse data sources, there's an increased focus on ethical AI and privacy. Techniques are being developed to ensure AI systems use data responsibly, respect privacy, and avoid biases.

Through these advancements, AI systems can now assimilate and analyze data from many sources, leading to more insightful, accurate, and comprehensive analyses and predictions. This capability is pivotal in fields ranging from healthcare and finance to environmental monitoring and smart cities.

4. Ability to store and retrieve massive amounts of data.

Artificial Intelligence (AI) systems handle the storage and retrieval of massive amounts of data through a combination of advanced technologies and methodologies.

- Distributed Computing: AI systems often use distributed computing environments, storing data across multiple machines or servers. This not only provides massive storage capacity but also enables parallel processing, which is crucial for quickly accessing and analyzing large datasets.

- Cloud Storage: Cloud platforms provide scalable, flexible, and efficient data storage solutions. They allow AI systems to access vast amounts of data from anywhere, at any time, without the need for local storage capacity. The cloud infrastructure is optimized for high-speed data retrieval and processing.

- Database Management Systems: Modern database management systems (DBMS) are designed to handle large volumes of data efficiently. These systems use advanced indexing, caching, and query optimization techniques to facilitate quick data retrieval.

- Data Warehousing and Data Lakes: AI systems often use data warehouses and data lakes to store structured and unstructured data, respectively. These systems are designed for high efficiency in data storage, management, and retrieval and support complex queries and analytics.

- In-Memory Computing: For immediate data processing, AI systems utilize in-memory computing. This approach stores data in RAM (Random Access Memory) instead of slower disk drives, allowing for much faster data access and processing.

- Big Data Technologies: Technologies like Hadoop and Spark are specifically designed for handling and processing big data. They allow for distributed storage and processing of large datasets, enabling AI systems to quickly access and analyze the data.

- Efficient Data Structures and Algorithms: AI systems use optimized data structures and algorithms specifically designed for fast data access and minimal storage requirements. For example, data may be stored in formats that are easy to compress and decompress or in structures that support rapid searches and updates.

- Caching Mechanisms: Caching is used to store frequently accessed data in a temporary storage area for quick retrieval. This reduces the time taken to fetch data from primary storage, especially if the same data is accessed repeatedly.

- Content Delivery Networks (CDNs): For AI applications that require the delivery of data over the internet, such as streaming services, CDNs are used. They store data in multiple, geographically distributed servers to ensure faster delivery and high availability.

- Hardware Optimizations: Specialized hardware like SSDs (Solid State Drives), GPUs (Graphics Processing Units), and TPUs (Tensor Processing Units) are often employed in AI systems. These hardware components are optimized for rapid data processing and can significantly speed up data retrieval and analysis.

By leveraging these technologies and methods, AI systems can effectively store, manage, and retrieve massive amounts of data almost instantly, enabling real-time analytics and decision-making in various applications.

5. Ability to "self-learn".

Self-learning in AI is a complex process that involves sophisticated algorithms, large datasets, and often significant computational resources. The ability of AI to self-learn and improve over time is what makes it particularly powerful for a wide range of applications. As mentioned earlier, Artificial Intelligence (AI) self-learning, often referred to as machine learning, particularly deep learning, involves algorithms that enable computers to learn from and make decisions based on data.

- Data Input: The self-learning process begins with data input. AI systems are exposed to substantial amounts of data, which could include text, images, videos, or any other form of data relevant to the task at hand.

- Feature Extraction: AI identifies, and extracts features from the input data. Features are individual measurable properties or characteristics of the phenomena being observed. For example, in image recognition, features might include edges, corners, or color distribution.

- Model Training: Using algorithms, the AI system processes the input data and learns from it by adjusting its internal parameters (such as weights in neural networks). This is often done through a process called training, where the algorithm iteratively improves its performance on a specific task.

- Supervised Learning: In supervised learning, the AI is trained on a labeled dataset, which means each data point is tagged with the correct answer. The model makes predictions during training and adjusts its parameters based on the accuracy of its predictions compared to the true labels.

- Unsupervised Learning: In unsupervised learning, the AI is given data without explicit instructions on what to do with it. The model tries to identify patterns and relationships in the data by itself, clustering comparable items together.

- Reinforcement Learning: In this type of learning, the AI learns by interacting with an environment. It makes decisions, receives feedback (rewards or penalties), and refines its strategies to achieve better outcomes or maximize a reward function.

- Pattern Recognition and Decision Making: Over time, the AI system learns to recognize patterns, make predictions, or take actions based on its training. The more data the AI is exposed to, the better it becomes at making accurate predictions or decisions.

- Continuous Learning and Adaptation: Some AI systems are designed for continuous learning, meaning they keep learning and adapting as new data comes in. This is particularly important for applications where the environment changes over time.

- Validation and Testing: To ensure that the AI system has learned effectively, it is tested on new, unseen data. This testing phase helps to evaluate the model's performance and generalizability.

- Feedback Loops: AI systems can be designed with feedback loops, where the output of the model is used to improve the system continuously. This is a form of self-optimization and is critical in applications where performance can be incrementally improved over time.

6. Advancements in artificial speech and recognition.

Advancements in artificial speech recognition have played a pivotal role in the growth and diversification of AI applications. Here's how these advancements have contributed.

- Improved Accuracy: Modern speech recognition systems have achieved elevated levels of accuracy, thanks to advances in deep learning and neural networks. This accuracy is crucial for applications like virtual assistants, automated customer service, and real-time transcription services.

- Understanding Context and Nuance: Advanced AI models can now understand context, accents, dialects, and nuances in speech, making them more reliable and versatile in different environments and for various user groups.

- Real-Time Processing: The ability to process speech in real-time has opened up new applications, such as real-time translation services, interactive language learning tools, and immediate voice command responses in smart devices and home automation systems.

- Expanded Accessibility: Speech recognition technology has greatly enhanced accessibility for individuals with disabilities. It enables voice-controlled interfaces and converts speech to text, assisting those with visual impairments or motor disabilities.

- Integration into Various Devices and Applications: Speech recognition is now integrated into a wide range of devices (like smartphones, smart speakers, and cars) and applications (such as search engines and navigation systems), making technology more interactive and user-friendly.

- Data Collection and Analysis: Improved speech recognition allows for more effective collection and analysis of voice data. This has applications in fields like healthcare for patient monitoring, in marketing for customer sentiment analysis, and security for voice biometrics.

- Enhancing Natural Language Understanding (NLU): Speech recognition advancements contribute to the broader field of NLU, helping AI better interpret and respond to human language, both spoken and written.

- Reducing the Language Barrier: AI's improved ability to recognize and process different languages and accents significantly reduces language barriers, facilitating global communication and collaboration.

- Cost Reduction and Efficiency: Automated speech recognition systems reduce the need for human transcriptionists in various fields, leading to cost savings and increased efficiency.

- Personalization and User Experience: AI can now learn individual speech patterns, accents, and preferences, leading to more personalized user experiences, especially in consumer products and services.

These advancements have not only made AI more accessible and user-friendly but have also expanded its capabilities and applications across different sectors, making it an integral part of modern technology and daily life.

Will AI ever reach "machine consciousness"?

The question of whether AI will ever achieve "machine consciousness" is both complex and speculative, involving a blend of technological, philosophical, and ethical considerations.

From a technological perspective, AI currently operates based on algorithms and data processing. Current AI systems lack self-awareness, emotions, subjective experiences, and consciousness as humans understand them. AI systems, including advanced ones like neural networks, function by identifying patterns in data and making decisions based on programming and learned information. This process, while sometimes mimicking aspects of human cognition, does not equate to consciousness.

Several challenges and considerations arise when discussing the potential for machine consciousness:

- Defining Consciousness: Consciousness in humans is not fully understood and is subject to extensive philosophical debate. Without a clear understanding of what consciousness is, replicating it in a machine becomes even more complex.

- Technological Limitations: Current AI technology operates within the realm of computational algorithms and lacks the autonomous, subjective experience that characterizes consciousness. Achieving consciousness would likely require a fundamental shift in the nature of AI technology, beyond what is currently known or theorized.

- Ethical and Moral Implications: The idea of a conscious machine raises significant ethical and moral questions. It challenges our understanding of rights and responsibilities and the nature of intelligence and consciousness.

- Philosophical and Theoretical Considerations: Some philosophers and scientists argue that consciousness is a uniquely biological phenomenon, inherently tied to living processes, which machines, as non-biological entities, would not be capable of achieving.

- Practicality and Purpose: From a practical standpoint, it's worth considering whether achieving machine consciousness is a desirable goal in AI development. AI's primary purpose is to augment and enhance human capabilities, and it's unclear how machine consciousness would contribute to this goal.

While AI continues to advance rapidly, achieving machine consciousness involves numerous unresolved technological, philosophical, and ethical challenges. As of now, it remains a speculative and theoretical concept rather than a tangible goal in AI research and development. The terms artificial general intelligence (AGI) and singularity have been discussed, expanding upon machine consciousness. Being aware of these two theories can help us better anticipate the future and perhaps better prepare for what might be a reality someday. Both AGI and Singularity will be further described in Chapter 8.

While 2023 was an amazing year for the growth in popularity of generative AI, most human interactions still relied on a keyboard as the central means of communication. Clearly, text-based communication is being replaced with actual voice interaction, where humans and machines communicate through oral speech. Many believe the machines we communicate with today will not only converse with us in our chosen language but will also become experts in reading our emotions, inflections, and unique nuances.

As we shall see, all forms of business and government have many opportunities to exploit this technology and provide better and more personalized services, when needed, in multiple languages. This text will aim to address the state and local government community and serve to help people better understand how this technology is already being applied and the many future possibilities that we either plan or dream of. We must also not forget the many inherent dangers that AI poses and how we humans can keep this technology in control. By the end of 2023, dozens of state and local governments developed both guidelines and policies aimed at the proper use of AI.

The Downside

Today's optimism and fascination with AI need to be tempered with the reality that there are inherent dangers in its use. It is critical that we be aware of the many roadblocks that lie ahead. We conclude this chapter with some of the larger concerns, hence the name "Downside." In Chapter One, we mentioned the inherent dangers of bias, but there is even more to be concerned with.

Errors & Hallucinations

At the time of this writing, generative AI is using generation 4, and there is every reason to believe there will be numerous and rapid updates. Many fail to understand that generative AI is programmed to anticipate the proper response as much as or more so than merely reciting back-stored information. This means that it can and has made mistakes. Worse, some of the mistakes look incredibly real and factual. This is called hallucinations.

An AI hallucination occurs when an artificial intelligence system generates or produces information, content, or responses that are not accurate, coherent, or relevant to the input or task at hand. It is akin to a human hallucination in the sense that it involves perceiving or generating something that is not grounded in reality or lacks a logical basis.

AI hallucinations can occur in various contexts, including natural language processing, image generation, and other machine-learning applications. They often arise when AI models generate outputs that are based on patterns learned from their training data but are not appropriate or accurate in the given context. These hallucinations can manifest as:

- Generating fake or false information: An AI might provide answers that sound plausible but are factually incorrect because it has learned incorrect information from its training data.

- Incoherent text generation: In natural language processing tasks, AI models may generate text that lacks coherence, makes no sense, or contradicts itself.

- Producing offensive or biased content: Some AI systems may produce content that is offensive, biased, or inappropriate due to biases in the training data.

- Creating surreal or nonsensical images: In image generation, AI systems may produce images that contain strange or unrealistic elements, creating a hallucinatory effect.

- Misinterpreting context: AI models might misunderstand the context of a conversation or task and generate responses that are unrelated or irrelevant to the user's input.

- Made-up information: AI has been known to completely make something up like a citation, a source, or what appears to be a fact that can be proven to be absolutely false. While some argue that generative AI systems have inherent flaws with dataset associations, others say they simply do not know the cause, hence an unsolved mystery.

AI hallucinations are a challenge in the field of artificial intelligence and machine learning, and efforts are ongoing to minimize these issues through improved training data, model architectures, and fine-tuning techniques to make AI systems more reliable and accurate in their responses.

AI Risks and Vulnerabilities

The known risks of AI are significant and can have far-reaching consequences. Chief among them is bias. Bias in AI systems can lead to unfair and discriminatory outcomes, reinforcing and perpetuating existing inequalities in society. Here are some of the key dangers associated with AI bias:

- Discrimination: AI bias can result in discriminatory outcomes, where certain groups of people are unfairly treated or disadvantaged based on their race, gender, age, or other characteristics. This can lead to real-world harm and exacerbate social inequalities.

- Unfair Opportunities: Bias in AI can affect opportunities in areas such as education, employment, housing, and finance, as AI systems may make biased decisions that limit access to resources and opportunities for certain groups.

- Reinforcing Stereotypes: Biased AI can reinforce harmful stereotypes by making decisions or predictions based on biased training data. This can perpetuate harmful beliefs and social norms.

- Loss of Privacy: Biased AI systems may also compromise individuals' privacy by making unfair and intrusive decisions, such as profiling or surveillance, based on inaccurate assumptions.

- Lack of Accountability: Bias in AI systems can make it challenging to assign responsibility for harmful outcomes, as it can be challenging to trace back to the specific source of bias in complex models. This lack of accountability can hinder efforts to rectify biases.

- Legal and Ethical Issues: AI bias can lead to legal and ethical challenges, with potential lawsuits and regulatory actions against organizations that deploy biased AI systems.

- Reduced Trust: When people perceive that AI systems are biased or unfair, it can erode trust in these technologies and hinder their widespread adoption and acceptance.

- Negative Feedback Loops: Biased AI can create feedback loops that reinforce existing inequalities. For example, if a biased AI system recommends job candidates based on historical hiring data, it may perpetuate a lack of diversity in the workplace.

- Economic Disparities: AI bias can exacerbate economic disparities by favoring certain groups in financial decisions, credit scoring, or loan approvals while disadvantaging others.

- Social and Political Instability: In extreme cases, AI bias can contribute to social unrest and political instability, particularly when marginalized groups experience discrimination or injustice due to biased AI systems.

To address these dangers, efforts are being made to develop AI algorithms that are more transparent, accountable, and fair. This includes improving data collection and preprocessing, auditing AI systems for bias, and implementing fairness-aware machine learning techniques. Ethical guidelines, regulations, and standards are also being developed to mitigate the risks associated with biased AI.

Privacy and AI?

Privacy risks associated with AI are a significant concern in today's data-driven world. As AI systems continue to collect, analyze, and utilize vast amounts of personal data, several privacy-related risks emerge:

- Data Breaches: AI relies on large datasets, and storing and processing such data carries a risk of data breaches. If unauthorized individuals or entities gain access to sensitive personal information, it can lead to identity theft, fraud, or other privacy violations.

- Data Misuse: AI systems can potentially misuse personal data by using it for purposes beyond the original intent or without individuals' consent. This can result in privacy violations and harm to individuals' rights.

- Profiling and Surveillance: AI can be used extensively for profiling and surveillance by governments and private entities.

- Advanced AI algorithms can analyze individuals' behavior, preferences, and online activities, leading to the creation of detailed profiles without their knowledge or consent.

- Facial Recognition: AI-powered facial recognition technology poses significant privacy risks by enabling the tracking and identification of individuals in public spaces without their consent. This can lead to mass surveillance and potential misuse by authorities or private companies.

- De-anonymization: AI can de-anonymize supposedly anonymous data by cross-referencing it with other available information, potentially revealing sensitive information about individuals who believed their data was protected.

- Inference Attacks: AI models can infer sensitive information about individuals by analyzing seemingly innocuous data. For example, an AI model might deduce someone's health condition or sexual orientation from their online behavior.

- Consent Challenges: AI can make it challenging to obtain informed consent from individuals, as they may not fully understand how their data will be used or the potential consequences. Complex AI algorithms may make it difficult to explain how decisions are made.

- Discriminatory Outcomes: AI-driven decisions can inadvertently result in discriminatory outcomes, even if no explicit personal data is used. This can affect employment, housing, and financial opportunities and perpetuate social inequalities.

- Data Retention: AI systems may store personal data for extended periods, increasing the risk of unauthorized access or misuse over time. Proper data retention policies and safeguards are necessary to mitigate this risk.

- Ethical Concerns: Privacy risks also extend to the ethical considerations surrounding AI and personal data. AI developers and organizations must grapple with questions of data ownership, consent, transparency, and accountability.

To address these privacy risks, it is crucial to implement robust data protection measures, adhere to privacy regulations (such as GDPR in Europe or CCPA in California), conduct privacy impact assessments, and adopt privacy-preserving AI techniques. Additionally, organizations and governments should prioritize privacy-aware AI development and promote public awareness about the importance of data privacy in the age of AI.

Copywrite

How do we know if an AI-generated response is taken from copyrighted work? Determining whether an AI-generated response is taken from copyrighted work can be challenging, as AI models like ChatGPT generate text based on patterns learned from a vast amount of data, which may include copyrighted materials. Here are some steps you can take to minimize the risk of using copyrighted content:

- Check for Proper Attribution: If the AI response contains a verbatim excerpt from a known copyrighted source, it should ideally include proper attribution to the original author or source. AI-generated content should not be presented as your own if it's derived from copyrighted material.

- Conduct a Plagiarism Check: Utilize plagiarism detection tools and software to analyze the text generated by the AI against known copyrighted works and publicly available content. These tools can help identify potential matches.

- Paraphrase and Cite Sources: If the AI response resembles a copyrighted work but is paraphrased or modified, ensure that you properly cite the original source to acknowledge the author's work.

- Verify the AI's Training Data: Understand the AI model's training data and the sources it has been exposed to. Some AI models have been trained on publicly available, non-copyrighted data, while others may have encountered copyrighted materials.

- Review AI's Content Policies: Check the terms of service and content usage policies of the AI platform you are using. Some platforms may have guidelines or restrictions regarding copyrighted material.

- Seek Legal Advice: If you are uncertain about the copyright status of AI-generated content or whether it infringes on copyright, consider consulting with a legal expert who specializes in intellectual property and copyright law.

It's important to note that AI-generated content can raise complex copyright and legal issues, and the interpretation of copyright law may vary by jurisdiction. To minimize risks, it's advisable to be cautious and take appropriate measures to ensure that you use AI-generated content in a legal and ethical manner, including proper attribution and citation when necessary. At the time of this manuscript, the US Copyright Office launched an investigation into AI and copyright and numerous lawsuits; most notably, The New York Times brought suit against ChatGPT, claiming copyright violations, as some noted authors claim the same.

AI and Humans

As we saw earlier in the chapter, policies are beginning to state things like 'we must learn to better communicate with machines' suggesting where AI is headed. Workers are beginning to feel a bit uneasy as they learn more about AI. Many workers are concerned about the potential impact on either their jobs or how they carry out their current tasks and responsibilities. State and local governments that have collective bargaining obligations are already addressing AI concerns. In the near future, AI is not expected to replace workers as much as it will augment tasks through AI-related automation, which can affect position descriptions and may require training or re-classification. As responsibilities change, so too will the accompanying expectations. The labor relation aspect of AI adoption will be watched very closely by both workers and management.

The succeeding chapters will dive a bit deeper and provide a more focused discussion of AI in state and local government while also providing useful considerations and, where appropriate, specific recommendations. Every day, we learn something new about AI, and this is about as good a starting point as any. This exciting journey continues, and it appears endless.

Chapter 2: Bibliography

https://www.techtarget.com/searchenterpriseai/tip/The-history-of-artificial-intelligence-Complete-AI-timeline

https://www.tableau.com/data-insights/ai/history

https://aws.amazon.com/what-is/artificial-general-intelligence/

https://ourworldindata.org/brief-history-of-ai

https://sitn.hms.harvard.edu/flash/2017/history-artificial-intelligence/

https://en.wikipedia.org/wiki/History_of_artificial_intelligence

https://cloud.google.com/learn/artificial-intelligence-vs-machine-learning

https://www.coursera.org/articles/machine-learning-vs-ai

https://ai.engineering.columbia.edu/ai-vs-machine-learning/

https://aws.amazon.com/compare/the-difference-between-artificial-intelligence-and-machine-learning/

https://ourworldindata.org/brief-history-of-ai

CHAPTER 3
Understanding AI In The Public Sector: Policies, Guidelines, And Governance

Absent any federal laws pertaining to AI regulations, state and local governments have actively been developing policies and guidelines, forming task groups, and creating AI centers of excellence. There is general agreement that now is the time to plan for appropriate AI usage.

How can local governments regulate generative AI?

Hardly a day goes by without some new warning or danger being reported about artificial intelligence (AI) and, in particular, generative AI. State and local governments have little choice but to confront AI with proactive policies regarding their usage policy given the vast amounts of personal data collected and stored on government systems.

The governor of Connecticut signed a bill into law calling for an AI Bill of Rights aimed at protecting citizens. The legislation follows a similar initiative from the White House, which presented a framework for an AI Bill of Rights at the federal level.

Professors across the nation worry that students will turn to generative AI to research and write class assignments and even dissertations.

To add to the growing list of warnings and concerns, the Federal Trade Commission (FTC) has opened an investigation into the company Open AI, which makes ChatGPT, over whether the chatbot has harmed consumers.

Public managers share many of the same concerns with private sector managers when it comes to limiting or even prohibiting workers from using generative AI at work. The shared concern is that employees will input sensitive information in return for the solutions they seek. The problem is that once data is entered into an open AI system, there is no control over what happens to the content and where and when such data might be shared with others.

Even the companies that offer generative AI cannot assure people what happens with any data entered into their systems. Ironically, they designed the very "black boxes" where no one knows what happens inside—not even the programmers. This growing list of concerns includes the fact that information that looks incredibly real and well-laid out without any typos can provide information and citations that are absolutely false. It did not take long for the term "hallucinations" to explain such phenomena.

Given generative AI's complexity, it is nearly impossible to identify the source(s) for data models, and all such systems lack transparency and accountability. Even sophisticated users have found it difficult, if not impossible, to assess the veracity of written reports and other forms of information. Complex algorithms are at the heart of today's generative AI systems, where there are inherent dangers in mixing reliable source data with bad data, with the possibility of promulgating unintended bias and/or prejudice. Worries extend to the protection of intellectual property and the possibility that bad actors (both domestic and international) could manipulate or manufacture data sources and propaganda, disinformation, or misinformation, adversely impacting public opinion, tilting an election, turning policies upside down—all of which would further erode public trust.

With so much at stake, governments at all levels struggle to create policies that offer legal remedies, the protection of privacy, and liabilities from unintended consequences. So, as a starting point, ChatGPT was asked, "How can local governments regulate generative AI?"

According to ChatGPT: "Regulating generative AI at the local government level can be a complex task, but here are some potential approaches that local governments can consider:

- Establishing ethical guidelines: Local governments can create ethical guidelines that outline the responsible use of generative AI technology. These guidelines can address issues such as bias, privacy, transparency, and accountability. They can provide a framework for developers and users to follow when creating or implementing generative AI systems.

- Licensing and certification: Governments can require individuals or organizations working with generative AI to obtain licenses or certifications. This process can involve demonstrating a certain level of understanding and adherence to ethical guidelines and best practices. Licensing and certification can help ensure that those developing and using generative AI technologies have the necessary expertise and are accountable for their actions.

- Data protection and privacy: Local governments can enact regulations to protect the privacy of individuals and the data used by generative AI systems. This can include requirements for obtaining explicit consent, secure data storage, and anonymization practices. These regulations can help mitigate privacy risks associated with generative AI applications.

- Algorithmic transparency: Local governments can advocate for transparency in generative AI algorithms. This can involve requiring developers and organizations to disclose information about the algorithms and data sources used in generative AI systems. Transparency measures can help uncover biases or potential ethical concerns associated with the outputs generated by AI systems.

- Public-private partnerships: Governments can collaborate with industry experts, researchers, and AI developers to develop standards and best practices for generative AI technology. By fostering collaboration between the public and private sectors, local governments can leverage the expertise of different stakeholders and develop effective regulations that balance innovation and societal impact.

- Testing and evaluation: Governments can establish testing and evaluation procedures to assess the performance, safety, and ethical implications of generative AI systems. These procedures can include audits, third-party assessments, and regular reporting to ensure compliance with regulations and guidelines.

- Public awareness and education: Local governments can play a crucial role in educating the public about generative AI technology, its potential benefits and risks. They can organize workshops, public forums, and awareness campaigns to help citizens understand the implications of generative AI and encourage responsible use.

It is important to note that the regulation of generative AI is a rapidly evolving field, and local governments should engage with experts, stakeholders, and the wider AI community to develop informed and effective regulatory approaches. Collaboration between various levels of government and international bodies can also help create consistent and globally harmonized regulations for generative AI."

Given ChatGPT's vast knowledge base, it is not particularly surprising that it provided the above outline for local governments to consider regarding what AI policies and regulations might contain. But one must ask, how was this outline developed? Sole source, multiple sources? While serving as a useful outline, sound policy development requires greater levels of detail and specifics. Here, policy development is still very much in the hands of humans. Clearly, there is so much more to learn about AI and ChatGPT; nonetheless, judging by its initial response to the question asked, this technology is already way ahead of humans.

Note: The above section of this chapter first appeared in American City & County Magazine, with permission, in July 2023.

State and local governments have tried to get ahead of AI use through developing policies and guidelines. Some states even banned generative AI until it could be further studied. The AI bills introduced at the state level differ from federal AI legislation in several ways. According to an analysis by BSA | The Software Alliance, the state legislation has surged, with a 440% increase in AI bill introductions in 2023 compared to the previous year. This state-based legislation reflects a broader effort by policymakers to set initial rules for AI systems, as federal legislation on AI is still nascent.

One key difference is that states have been more proactive in addressing AI regulation, with many states introducing bills focused on specific AI use cases, AI governance frameworks, AI use inventories, task forces and committees, law enforcement use of AI tools, and state governments' use of AI. In contrast, federal legislation has been slower to materialize, with the American Data Protection and Privacy Act (ADPPA) stalling during the past Congressional session.

Furthermore, state legislation has focused on addressing a wide array of concerns, such as privacy, bias, discrimination, safety, and security, among other topics. States have also been active in regulating specific AI applications, such as mental health services, deepfakes, and automated decision-making. In contrast, federal legislation has primarily focused on government AI systems.

In the 2023 legislative session, at least 25 states, Puerto Rico, and the District of Columbia introduced artificial intelligence bills. Here is a listing of several states in the U.S. that have passed AI policies or guidelines. Some of the key states include:

Illinois: In 2019, Illinois became the first state to enact restrictions on the use of AI in hiring. The Illinois AI Video Interview Act was amended in 2021 and went into effect in 2022, requiring employers using AI-enabled assessments to notify applicants of AI use, explain how the AI works, and obtain their consent.

California: California has proposed several bills related to AI regulation, such as AB1502, which aims to prevent healthcare providers using automated decision systems from discriminating based on numerous factors, and S313, which would require any state agency using generative AI to disclose its use.

New Jersey: New Jersey has proposed a bill (SB3876) to appoint an Artificial Intelligence Officer to oversee state agencies' use of AI.

New York: New York has also proposed a bill (A5309) that would require state units to purchase products that use automated decision-making to adhere to responsible AI.

Washington: Washington has proposed a bill (S5356) that would regulate the use of automated decision tools in employment.

Rhode Island: S117, which would establish a commission to study and regulate the state government's use of AI, and H6423, which requests that the government review the extent of automated decision-making used by the state.

North Carolina: S460, which would establish a committee on automation and the workforce.

Pennsylvania: HB49, which would create a registry of all businesses using AI in the state, and HR170/SR143, which urges the state to establish an advisory committee to investigate AI's impacts on the state.

Texas: H3633, which would establish a committee to decide whether to establish a program to train individuals for the workforce.

These are just a few examples. Several other states have either passed or proposed AI-related legislation, reflecting the increasing focus on AI regulation at the state level.

Local governments have been quite busy passing laws and guidelines of their own. Local governments increasingly leverage AI to improve efficiency, enhance citizen services, and drive innovation. AI algorithms can efficiently analyze large volumes of data, providing valuable insights and facilitating evidence-based decision-making. By analyzing complex datasets, AI can help identify emerging issues, predict potential problems, and streamline the decision-making process. Additionally, AI implementation in local government can automate administrative tasks, enhance the quality and effectiveness of city services, and improve citizen interactions through AI-powered chatbots.

However, implementing AI in local government is not without its challenges. One major hurdle is the initial cost associated with the adoption and implementation of AI technologies. Furthermore, ensuring transparency, accountability, and fairness in using AI systems, as well as addressing concerns related to data privacy and security, are crucial to maintaining public trust.

Local governments are also focusing on establishing clear goals and objectives for AI projects, developing collaborative partnerships for AI initiatives, evaluating and measuring the impact of AI solutions, and ensuring the ethical and responsible use of AI technologies. By doing so, they aim to empower themselves to tackle complex challenges and pave the way for smarter, more sustainable communities.

Overall, local governments are embracing AI technologies responsibly and strategically to improve decision-making processes, optimize service delivery, enhance citizen satisfaction, and foster more sustainable and livable cities.

State Centers of Excellence in AI

To date, there are at least four states that have created state centers of excellence in AI; they are New York, California, Texas, and Virginia. The mission of these centers is to accelerate research, innovation, and adoption of artificial intelligence (AI) technologies. Such efforts are designed to help support state and local governments and public institutions of higher education to explore artificial intelligence (AI) technologies and to foster digital transformation. The State of Virginia announced that it will offer a suite of AI services to state agencies. New York State has created a well-funded consortium consisting of all the major universities housed at the University of Buffalo. In California, The California Department of Technology has created the Artificial Intelligence Community (AIC). The mission of the AIC is to bring state experts together to shape the future of ethical, transparent, and trustworthy artificial intelligence.

Each of the state efforts recognizes that AI has the potential to create significant opportunities for government transformation, enabling greater efficiency while improving the accuracy and effectiveness of decision-making and service delivery.

The first round of state action centered around either slowing down AI usage or setting up a mechanism for further study leading to action. These efforts generally took place in 2022 and early 2023. In 2024, state governments are planning a much greater proactive role in promoting innovation through responsible AI.

Guidelines or Policy?

Some cities and counties have established guidelines for AI use for their employees, both personally and for the creation or acquisition of AI-generated applications and or services. Others have developed policies first with the idea of creating guidelines as the next step. The question is does it matter which comes first, policy or guidelines? Those who have developed guidelines first explain that this provides the flexibility to modify or change given the extremely fast-moving pace of AI developments.

AI guidelines for state and local governments typically encompass a set of principles and recommendations to govern the development, deployment, and use of artificial intelligence technologies within their jurisdictions. These guidelines often include the following key aspects:

- Ethical and Responsible AI: This section emphasizes the ethical use of AI systems, including fairness, accountability, transparency, and privacy considerations.

- Human-Centered Design: Prioritizing AI systems that enhance human capabilities, promote inclusivity, and address societal needs.

- Data Governance: Establishing policies for responsible data collection, management, and use, including data privacy protections and safeguards against bias and discrimination.

- Accountability and Oversight: Implementing mechanisms for accountability, such as audibility, explainability, and recourse mechanisms for individuals affected by AI systems.

- Collaboration and Stakeholder Engagement: Encouraging collaboration among government agencies, industry stakeholders, academia, and civil society to develop and implement AI policies that serve public interests.

- Risk Management and Mitigation: Identifying potential risks associated with AI deployment, such as cybersecurity threats, job displacement, and societal impacts, and implementing measures to mitigate these risks.

- Compliance with Legal and Regulatory Frameworks: Ensuring that AI initiatives comply with existing laws, regulations, and standards, including those related to privacy, civil rights, and data protection.

- Education and Training: Promoting AI literacy and providing training for government officials and staff to better understand AI technologies and their implications.

- Public Engagement and Transparency: Fostering transparency and public trust through open communication, public consultations, and accessible information about government AI initiatives.

- Continuous Improvement and Evaluation: Establishing mechanisms for ongoing monitoring, evaluation, and adaptation of AI policies and practices to address emerging challenges and opportunities.

These guidelines, as an example, serve as a framework for state and local governments to navigate the complexities of AI governance and ensure that AI technologies are deployed in a manner that benefits society while minimizing potential risks and harms.

Policies are usually approved by a governing body such as a city council. While the terms "guidelines" and "policies" are sometimes used interchangeably, they can have distinct connotations in the context of governance frameworks.

While AI guidelines provide general principles and recommendations for ethical and responsible AI development and deployment, AI policies are more formal and specific regulations or rules that dictate how AI technologies should be used within a governmental context. Here's how they contrast:

1. Scope and Specificity:

- Guidelines: AI guidelines are often broad and high-level, providing general principles and recommendations without specifying detailed requirements or enforcement mechanisms.

- Policies: AI policies are more specific and detailed, outlining concrete rules, regulations, and procedures for the development, deployment, and use of AI technologies within a governmental context.

2. Flexibility vs. Enforcement:

- Guidelines: AI guidelines offer flexibility, allowing governments to adapt and interpret the principles based on their specific needs and contexts. Compliance with guidelines is often voluntary, although adherence may be encouraged through various means.

- Policies: AI policies are typically mandatory and enforceable, with clear expectations and consequences for non-compliance. They may include legal frameworks, regulatory requirements, and oversight mechanisms to ensure adherence. 3. Legal Status:

- Guidelines: AI guidelines may lack legal enforceability, serving more as best practices or recommendations for governments to consider when developing their own AI policies.

- Policies: AI policies have legal standing and are binding within the jurisdiction they govern. Violations of AI policies may result in legal penalties or sanctions. 4. Development Process:

- Guidelines: AI guidelines are often developed through collaborative processes involving stakeholders from government, industry, academia, and civil society. They may be periodically updated to reflect evolving technology and societal norms.

- Policies: AI policies are typically developed through formal legislative or regulatory processes, involving drafting, public consultation, review, and approval by relevant authorities.

Overall, while AI guidelines provide overarching principles and guidance for ethical AI development and deployment, AI policies establish concrete rules and regulations to govern the use of AI within specific governmental contexts.

Both are essential components of a comprehensive AI governance framework, with guidelines informing the development of policies and policies providing the necessary legal and regulatory framework for implementation.

Tempe, AZ, was the first city in the state and one of the first nationally to develop an Ethical Artificial Intelligence (AI) Policy in May 2023. The city council unanimously passed it, and it is presented here as an example.

City of Tempe Arizona, USA

Ethical Artificial Intelligence (AI) Policy

(May 31, 2023)

I.   Purpose

The City of Tempe established the Ethical Artificial Intelligence (AI) Policy to affirm Tempe's commitment to responsible and ethical use of AI through the principles that ensure transparency, fairness, accountability, and the protection of individual rights in all AI-related activities conducted by the City of Tempe. Being intentional in our adoption and use of AI technologies will drive innovation and support increased efficiencies in operations and improved experiences for community engagement. This policy outlines the principles, guidelines, and procedures governing the responsible and ethical use of AI technologies within Tempe.

II.   Scope

This policy applies to the design, development, and deployment of AI for:

•   All departments, agencies, employees, contractors, and stakeholders involved in the development, deployment, and utilization of AI within Tempe.

•   Categories of AI inclusive of predictive analytics, machine learning, deep learning, generative AI, and automated decision-making

•   All cases where AI functionality is known to be included, such as new tools for existing products, new products being considered for use or where AI technology is developed by Tempe employees, contractors, partner agencies or other stakeholders.

III.   Policy Statement

The City of Tempe is committed to designing, developing, and deploying AI technologies in a responsible and ethical manner. We recognize that AI has the potential to significantly impact society and drive innovation, and we believe that it is our duty to ensure that its development, adoption, and use align with the principles of fairness, transparency, accountability, and respect for human rights. With this in mind, we hereby establish our ethical AI policy, outlining the principles and guidelines that will govern our AI initiatives:

1. Purpose and Scope. We will clearly define the problem the AI technology would solve including the purpose and the scope of application.

2. Human-Centered Approach: We will prioritize the well-being, safety, and dignity of individuals and communities affected by AI technology we use. We will strive to understand and address the needs and values of humans, promoting AI technologies that enhance human capabilities, foster inclusion, and contribute to the overall betterment of society.

3. Human Responsibility: We will clearly define the roles and responsibilities of human operators in utilizing AI systems, including their training requirements and obligations for monitoring, and intervening in system decisions.

4. Human-AI Collaboration: We will encourage collaboration between humans and AI systems, leveraging the strengths of both to enhance decision-making processes and ensure that ultimate control remains with humans.

5. Fairness and Avoidance of Bias: We will actively work to eliminate biases and ensure fairness in our design, development, and deployment of AI technology. We will take steps to prevent discrimination, protect privacy, and mitigate the risks of unfair or unjust outcomes resulting from AI algorithms. We will continuously assess and mitigate potential biases throughout the AI lifecycle.

6. Transparency and Explainability: We will strive to make our selection, design, development, and deployment of AI technology transparent and explainable to the best of our abilities. We will clearly disclose where individuals are interacting with AI or interacting with AI generated content. We will provide clear documentation and accessible information about the functioning and purpose of the AI technologies we use, enabling users, stakeholders and those who are subject to decisions informed by AI to understand and question the decision-making processes involved.

7. Accountability and Oversight: We will establish standards for accountability and oversight throughout the selection, design, development, and deployment of AI technology. We will be responsible for the actions and impacts of the AI technology we use, and we will implement strategies to identify, mitigate and rectify any potential harms or unintended consequences resulting from their use. We will proactively engage in ongoing monitoring, evaluation, and auditing to ensure compliance with ethical standards.

8. Data Privacy and Security: We will maintain the highest standards of data privacy and security in our AI initiatives. We will handle personal data in accordance with applicable policy, laws, and regulations, and we will implement robust safeguards to protect data from unauthorized access, misuse, or breaches.

9. Collaboration and Public Engagement: We will actively engage with stakeholders, such as users, experts, policymakers, and community organizations, to solicit diverse perspectives and feedback on the AI technology under consideration or currently used. We will seek to foster collaboration and share knowledge to address ethical challenges and ensure that AI technologies benefit society as a whole.

10. Continuous Monitoring and Ethical Improvement: We will continuously strive to improve the ethical aspects of our AI technology through research, innovation, and learning from our experiences. We will keep abreast of emerging ethical guidelines and best practices, adapting our policies and practices accordingly.

11. Training Programs: We will provide training programs and resources to employees involved in AI system development and utilization, promoting AI literacy, ethical considerations, privacy protection, and responsible AI practices.

12. Compliance and Legal Frameworks: We will comply with applicable laws, standards, and regulations related to AI and data protection. We will actively support the development of ethical AI regulations and frameworks that align with our principles and contribute to the responsible use of AI technology.

This ethical AI policy statement reflects our commitment to responsible and ethical AI. We recognize that ethical considerations are paramount, and we will hold ourselves accountable to these principles as we work towards creating AI technologies that benefit humanity and contribute positively to our collective future.

IV.   AI Governance

1. Departments shall

a) Define clear objectives and goals in support of adopting an AI solution and the intended use(s) of the solution.

b) Collaborate with Information Technology to complete the Artificial Intelligence Review process and will implement any mitigation strategies identified during the review.

c) Conduct semiannual reviews of implemented AI solutions. 2. Technology and Innovation Steering Committee shall

a) Establish mechanisms for ongoing monitoring and evaluation of AI solutions to ensure compliance with this policy and relevant laws and regulations.

b) Develop reporting mechanisms for AI-related activities, including regular audits to assess policy compliance and identify areas for improvement.

c) Define consequences for non-compliance with this policy, including disciplinary actions or contract termination, and establish remedial measures to address violations or failures of AI systems.

d) Support public awareness campaigns and educational initiatives to inform and engage the public on AI-related activities, their purpose, and potential impacts.

3. Information Technology shall

a) Collaborate with departments to develop the Artificial Intelligence Review Process.

b) Collaborate with departments to complete the Artificial Intelligence Review process and semiannual review.

c) Provide training programs and resources to employees involved in AI system development and utilization, promoting AI literacy, ethical considerations, privacy protection, and responsible AI practices.

This policy will be periodically reviewed and updated as necessary to address emerging challenges, technological advancements, and changes in legal or regulatory frameworks related to AI.

One area of their policy that truly stands out is the section headed Human-AI Collaboration, which states, "We will encourage collaboration between humans and AI systems, leveraging the strengths of both to enhance decision-making processes and ensure that ultimate control remains with humans." Clearly, this policy recognizes and anticipates the growing human-machine relationship that some now refer to as human-machine partnership. This item is far-reaching and recognizes where we are headed with AI systems.

It is worth highlighting the City of San Jose, which issued a 23-page comprehensive Generative AI Guidelines in July 2023.

New York City, taking a more surgical approach, established an Automated Decision Systems Task Force to examine how algorithms are used in city government and to develop recommendations for more transparent and equitable practices. The task force's work led to the creation of a first-of-its-kind algorithmic transparency bill requiring the city to disclose information about the automated decision systems it uses.

The State of Massachusetts released a set of AI principles aimed at guiding the ethical development and use of AI technologies by state agencies. The principles emphasize transparency, accountability, fairness, and public engagement in AI initiatives, reflecting a commitment to responsible AI governance.

While states and cities work on AI policies and guidelines, many are looking to the federal government for leadership and overall guidance. In late 2023, the President issued an *Executive Order on the Safe, Secure, and Trustworthy Development and Use of Artificial Intelligence.* This massive order went further than any previous executive order related to AI. The Presidential Order on AI, issued in 2023, focuses on promoting the safe, secure, and trustworthy development and use of artificial intelligence. The main points of the order include:

1. Safety and Security: The order promotes the development and implementation of repeatable processes and mechanisms to understand and mitigate risks related to AI adoption, including

biosecurity, cybersecurity, national security, and critical infrastructure.

2. Innovation and Competition: It compels actions to attract AI talent to the United States, understand novel intellectual property questions, protect inventors and creators, and promote AI innovation, including at startups and small businesses.

3. Worker Support: The order directs agencies to research and develop potential mitigations against disruptions to the workforce caused by AI adoption.

4. Consideration of AI Bias and Civil Rights: It addresses the perpetuation of biases by AI models and their potential impact on civil rights, including equity and civil rights considerations for the use of AI in the criminal justice system and the administration of federal government programs and benefits.

5. Consumer Protection: The order instructs agencies to enforce existing authorities to minimize consumer harm and identify needed authorities related to AI.

6. Privacy: It calls for the evaluation and mitigation of privacy risks associated with the collection, use, and retention of user data, potentially exacerbated by AI.

7. Federal Use of AI: The order requires the establishment of an interagency council to coordinate AI use by federal agencies and develop guidance on AI governance and risk management activities for agencies. It also acknowledges the ubiquity of generative AI tools and directs agencies to move toward adoption with safeguards in place.

8. International Leadership: The order declares that the United States should be a global leader in AI development and adoption by engaging with international allies and partners, leading efforts to develop common AI regulatory and accountability principles, and advancing responsible global technical standards for AI.

The order also includes specific directives related to various aspects of AI, such as the development of standards, tools, and tests to ensure the safety and security of AI systems, as well as measures to protect Americans from AI-enabled fraud and deception.

Finally, the order directs each federal agency to establish a Chief AI Officer. Additionally, it outlines actions to ensure responsible government deployment of AI, advance American leadership abroad, and reduce risks at the intersection of AI and CBRN (chemical, biological, radiological, and nuclear) threats.

The Chief AI Officer (CAIO)

Late last year the White House issued an Executive Order on the *Safe, Secure, and Trustworthy Development and Use of Artificial Intelligence*. On page 52 of the massive 66-page document, the Executive Order (EO) called for each Federal Agency to establish a permanent Chief AI Officer. The EO specifies the primary responsibility, in coordination with other responsible officials, for coordinating their agency's use of AI, promoting AI innovation in their agency, managing risks from their agency's use of AI, and promoting the use of trustworthy artificial intelligence in the Federal Government. While this has no direct bearing on state and local government it does serve as a blueprint for AI governance. What makes this position so remarkable is the fact that AI was hardly on anyone's radarscope some 5 years ago. Prior to the Executive Order, a few states had already assigned senior-level people to manage and coordinate AI initiatives - and local governments were not far behind. Given the history of federal initiatives, what happens at the federal government often gets adopted by state and local governments in some form or fashion.

The role of the Chief AI Officer (CAIO) is designed to play an increasingly significant role in both the private and public sectors. The CAIO is responsible for overseeing the development and implementation of AI technologies across the federal government. The massive AI executive Order failed to spell out the actual duties and expectations of the required CAIO. While we can expect to see further clarification of the roles and responsibilities of the CAIO, one can easily create a listing of roles and responsibilities which would include:

1. Strategic Leadership and Vision:
   - Developing and leading the organization's AI strategy to support its overall government's goals.

   - Ensuring the alignment of AI initiatives with the organization's strategic objectives.

   - Advocating for and communicating the value of AI investments to stakeholders at all levels, including elected leaders, public managers, employees, and external business partners.

2. AI Governance and Ethics:
   - Establishing governance structures to oversee AI projects, ensuring they adhere to ethical standards and comply with relevant laws and regulations.

- Implementing frameworks for responsible AI use, including transparency, fairness, accountability, and privacy.

3. Innovation and Transformation:
   - Identifying opportunities for AI to create value, improve efficiency, and drive innovation within the organization.

   - Leading digital transformation initiatives, leveraging AI to enhance products, services, and customer experiences.

   - Monitors AI use across all lines of government businesses.

4. Collaboration and Partnerships:

   - Fostering collaboration across departments (e.g., IT, operations, government branding, HR) to ensure AI projects meet business and operational needs.

   - Building and maintaining relationships with external partners, vendors, and the AI research community to stay ahead of technological advancements.

5. Talent Management and Development: Attracting, retaining, and developing AI talent, including data scientists, machine learning engineers, and other specialists.

   - Promoting an organizational culture that supports continuous learning and adaptation in the face of AI-driven change.

6. Data and Technology Management:

   - Overseeing the development and maintenance of the data infrastructure required to support AI initiatives.

- Ensuring the organization has the necessary technology and tools to develop, deploy, and scale AI solutions effectively.

- Ensuring AI systems are well-maintained and protected against cyber threats.

7. Risk Management and Compliance:

- Identifying and mitigating risks associated with AI, including technological, reputational, and operational risks.

- Ensuring AI projects comply with data protection laws, intellectual property rights, and industry-specific regulations.

- Ensuring AI disclosure is clearly stated on any AI-generated reports, publications, and data.

8. Performance Measurement and Improvement:

- Establishing metrics and KPIs to measure the effectiveness and impact of AI initiatives.

- Regularly reviewing and adjusting AI strategies based on performance data and changing business needs.

9. Training and Development:

- Provide AI training to all government employees to help them understand the appropriate use of the technology and its potential for misuse.

- Provide professional development access to external AI programs.

- Conduct AI best practice awards for AI adoption.

- Develop a culture of sharing best practices in the innovative use of AI.

10. Public Outreach:

- Keep the public and community interest groups appraised of AI use in government.

- Serve as the principal spokesperson on all AI-related issues.

With the CAIO position now required in federal agencies, state and local governments can learn from the experiences at the federal level. For smaller states and local governments, the issue will be, "Can we afford a new senior hire"? State and local governments have three basic choices; do nothing for now, hire a CAIO, or parcel out the main responsibilities among existing staff. Looking at the model of the 10 responsibilities one can divide these responsibilities into 5 categories, which could be:

- Technology (CIO? CTO?)
- Policy & Guidelines (Staff Attorney? Committee?)
- Human Resources and Training (Training Manager? HR Director?)
- Leadership (CAO? Deputy?)
- Communications (internal & external) (Communications Director, PIO? PR?)

As AI continues to evolve and its applications become more widespread, the role of the Chief AI Officer, whether in title or function, will expand and adapt in response to unfolding new challenges and opportunities. Ideally, the CAIO can and will play a critical role in ensuring that AI technologies are leveraged in a way that is strategic and ethical and maximizes value for the organization.

Regarding the issue of leadership, the question of reporting relationships and hierarchy needs to be determined. Who does the CAIO report to or through? Should it be the CIO; the chief administrative officer, or someone else?

Note: The CAIO section of this chapter first appeared in American City & County Magazine, with permission, in February 2024.

Auditing AI

Given all of the focus on explainable AI, ethics, and bias, the concept of AI audits has become a new area of inquiry. In June 2021, the federal government's General Accountability Office (GAO) developed a report, *Artificial Intelligence: An Accountability Framework for Federal Agencies and Other Entities*. This was the first known framework for AI in government.

This groundbreaking report identified key accountability practices—centered around the principles of governance, data, performance, and monitoring—to help federal agencies and others use AI responsibly. For example, the governance principle calls for users to set clear goals and engage with diverse stakeholders.

An AI audit involves a comprehensive assessment of artificial intelligence systems to ensure their safety, legality, and ethics. Key aspects of AI auditing include assessing the system's efficacy, reliability, and security to prevent failures and vulnerabilities. AI audits aim to map out risks in technical functionality and governance structures and recommend measures for improvement and compliance.

Today an AI audit is viewed as a comprehensive evaluation of an organization's artificial intelligence systems, processes, and data that ensures compliance, accuracy, fairness, and ethical considerations. Here's an outline of what an AI audit might involve:

1. **Scope Definition**: Define the scope of the audit, including the AI systems, algorithms, models, and datasets to be evaluated. Determine the objectives of the audit, such as ensuring compliance with regulations, assessing model performance, or identifying ethical risks.

2. **Data Collection and Review**: Gather information about the AI systems under review, including documentation, code, algorithms, datasets, and relevant policies and procedures. Review the data sources and data collection methods to ensure data quality, relevance, and appropriateness.

3. **Algorithm and Model Evaluation**:

   - Assess the design and implementation of algorithms and models, including their architecture, parameters, and training procedures.

- Evaluate model performance metrics such as accuracy, precision, recall, F1 score, bias, fairness, and robustness.
- Investigate the impact of model outputs on different demographic groups to identify potential biases or discrimination.

4. **Ethical and Regulatory Compliance**:

- Evaluate the AI systems for compliance with relevant laws, regulations, and ethical guidelines, such as GDPR, CCPA, HIPAA, or industry-specific standards.
- Assess the transparency and explainability of AI systems to ensure they can be understood and interpreted by stakeholders.
- Identify and address potential ethical risks, such as privacy violations, algorithmic bias, or unintended consequences.

5. **Risk Assessment and Mitigation**:

- Conduct a risk assessment to identify potential risks associated with the AI systems, including legal, financial, reputational, and ethical risks.
- Develop strategies to mitigate identified risks, such as improving data quality, enhancing model transparency, or implementing fairness-aware algorithms.

6. **Documentation and Reporting**:

- Document the findings of the audit, including strengths, weaknesses, and areas for improvement.
- Prepare a comprehensive audit report summarizing the audit process, findings, recommendations, and action plan for addressing identified issues.
- Communicate the results of the audit to relevant stakeholders, including senior management, regulatory authorities, and data subjects.

7. **Continuous Monitoring and Improvement**:

- Implement mechanisms for ongoing monitoring and evaluation of AI systems to ensure compliance, accuracy, and fairness over time.
- Establish processes for periodic audits and reviews to address emerging risks and changes in regulatory requirements or business operations.
- Continuously improve AI governance practices, including data management, model development, and ethical considerations, based on audit findings and industry best practices.

Overall, an AI audit is a systematic process aimed at assessing the performance, compliance, and ethical implications of AI systems to ensure they operate responsibly and responsibly. It seems reasonable to assume that AI audits will grow in importance and quite possibly become a legal requirement in the coming years.

Chapter 3: Bibliography

https://www.americancityandcounty.com/2023/07/19/how-can-local-governments-regulate-generative-ai-just-ask-chatgpt/

https://dir.texas.gov/strategic-digital-services/initiatives/artificial-intelligence-ai-center-excellence

https://statetechmagazine.com/article/2021/11/virginia-offer-suite-ai-services-state-agencies

https://www.buffalo.edu/news/releases/2024/01/hochul-empire-ai-ub.html

https://cdt.ca.gov/technology-innovation/artificial-intelligence-community/

https://www.whitehouse.gov/briefing-room/statements-releases/2023/10/30/fact-sheet-president-biden-issues-executive-order-on-safe-secure-and-trustworthy-artificial-intelligence/

https://www.whitehouse.gov/briefing-room/presidential-actions/2023/10/30/executive-order-on-the-safe-secure-and-trustworthy-development-and-use-of-artificial-intelligence/

https://crsreports.congress.gov/product/pdf/R/R47843

https://www.ey.com/en_us/public-policy/key-takeaways-from-the-biden-administration-executive-order-on-ai

https://news.usni.org/2023/11/21/highlights-of-the-2023-executive-order-on-artificial-intelligence

https://www.brennancenter.org/our-work/research-reports/states-take-lead-regulating-artificial-intelligence

https://www.bclplaw.com/en-US/events-insights-news/2023-state-by-state-artificial-intelligence-legislation-snapshot.html

https://epic.org/the-state-of-state-ai-laws-2023/

https://www.ncsl.org/technology-and-communication/artificial-intelligence-2023-legislation

https://www.brookings.edu/articles/why-states-and-localities-are-acting-on-ai/

https://www.ncsl.org/technology-and-communication/artificial-intelligence-2023-legislation

https://www.americancityandcounty.com/2024/02/13/the-chief-artificial-intelligence-officer-a-blueprint-for-state-and-local-government/

https://www.gao.gov/products/gao-21-519sp

https://censius.ai/wiki/ai-audit

https://www.holisticai.com/blog/ai-auditing

https://nanonets.com/blog/using-artificial-intelligence-in-audits/

https://www.law.com/legaltechnews/2023/10/20/navigating-the-ai-audit-a-comprehensive-guide-to-best-practices/

https://ec.europa.eu/futurium/en/system/files/ged/auditing-artificial-intelligence.pdf

CHAPTER 4
All Things Data

Governments at all levels collect vast amounts of data from the moment we are born. The volume of data collected by the federal government alone is immense, encompassing everything from census information and tax records to surveillance data and intelligence reports. With the advent of digital technologies and the increasing use of electronic records, the amount of data collected and stored has grown exponentially over the years.

Overall, it can be said with confidence that the federal government manages petabytes or even exabytes of data, given its vast array of responsibilities and activities. State and local governments also collect vast amounts of data.

When you think about it, it is the business of the government to collect and analyze data, whereas, in comparison, the private sector collects only a fraction of what the government amasses. In today's environment, the government, along with the private sector, collects trillions of pieces of data every day, which can take the form of structured, unstructured, and even social media sources.

Like the octopus on the book's cover, AI is powerless without data and AI has its tentacles in all forms of data, structured, unstructured, and social media. Experts advise that a key prerequisite is to focus on data classification and governance.

Data and artificial intelligence (AI) are interrelated fields, with data serving as the fuel that powers AI systems. The key elements of data and AI include:

- Data Collection: This involves gathering raw information from various sources such as sensors, databases, social media, and others. The quality, quantity, and variety of data collected are crucial for effective AI implementation.

- Data Storage and Management: Once collected, data needs to be stored in a structured manner that allows for easy access and retrieval. Data management also involves tasks such as cleaning, processing, and transforming raw data into a usable format.

- Data Preprocessing: Raw data often contains errors, missing values, and inconsistencies. Data preprocessing techniques such as cleaning, normalization, and feature engineering prepare the data for analysis by AI algorithms.

- Feature Extraction: Feature extraction involves selecting or extracting relevant features from the most informative data for the AI model. This step helps reduce dimensionality and focus on the most important aspects of the data.

- Machine Learning Algorithms: Machine learning algorithms are used to train AI models to learn patterns and relationships from data. These algorithms include supervised, unsupervised, and reinforcement learning techniques.

- Model Training: In this step, AI models are trained on labeled data (supervised learning) or unlabeled data (unsupervised learning) to make predictions or decisions.

- Evaluation and Validation: After training, AI models need to be evaluated and validated using separate datasets to ensure they generalize well to new, unseen data. Performance metrics such as accuracy, precision, recall, and F1-score are commonly used to evaluate AI models.

- Deployment and Integration: Once validated, AI models are deployed into production environments where they can make predictions or decisions in real time. Integration with existing systems and processes is essential for seamless deployment.

- Monitoring and Maintenance: AI models need to be continuously monitored in production to ensure they are performing as expected. This involves monitoring key performance indicators (KPIs), detecting drift, and retraining models as needed to maintain accuracy and reliability.

- Ethical and Regulatory Considerations: Data and AI applications raise important ethical and regulatory considerations regarding privacy, bias, fairness, transparency, and accountability. Addressing these considerations throughout the data and AI lifecycle is essential.

These elements form the foundation of data-driven AI systems and are essential for effectively leveraging data to create intelligent solutions. Of course, this leads to the need to better understand data quality, data organization, data location, and data governance.

Data Quality - Garbage In Garbage Out

The expression "garbage in garbage out" has been used to illustrate the fact that data outcomes are only as good as their inputs. AI systems have been trained using, in particular, large language models, to digest millions of articles, papers, and books – just about everything that has been indexed and stored through the Internet and private databases. It is no wonder some results are biased, misleading, or completely inaccurate. Given the unimaginable speed of data ingestion of today's AI systems programmers continue to work on methods to fact-check or analyze through select filters. Newer versions of generative AI applications can now provide citations and references for where certain data originated.

- Lack of Transparency: Closed AI systems may lack transparency regarding their inner workings, training data, or decision-making processes, raising concerns about accountability, bias, and ethical implications.

- Innovation Constraints: Closed AI systems may limit innovation by preventing collaboration, knowledge sharing, and exchanging ideas and resources with the broader research community.

- Vendor Lock-in: Closed AI systems may lead to vendor lock-in, where organizations become dependent on specific providers or technologies, limiting flexibility and freedom of choice.

- Cost and Resources: Closed AI systems may require significant investment in cost, time, and resources for development, deployment, and maintenance, which can be prohibitive for some organizations or industries.

In summary, both open and closed AI systems have their own sets of advantages and disadvantages, and the choice between them depends on several factors, including the specific use case, organizational requirements, ethical considerations, and regulatory compliance.

Data Organization Optimized for AI

Before feeding data into AI models, it often needs to be preprocessed. This may involve tasks such as cleaning, normalization, feature scaling, and handling missing values to improve the quality and usability of the data. Data integration is another aspect of data organization. AI systems often require data from multiple sources. Integrating diverse data sources seamlessly ensures that the AI model can access all relevant information for analysis and decision-making. Finally, as data volumes grow, AI systems must be designed to scale efficiently. Employing distributed computing, parallel processing, and optimized algorithms can improve performance and scalability for handling large datasets.

Data Location

A critical component of sound data management is knowing where data is stored. Data is usually stored in on-premises data centers, data lakes, data warehouses, and cloud-based data solutions. Each type of data storage solution has its advantages and trade-offs, and the choice depends on factors such as data volume, structure, access patterns, performance requirements, and scalability needs. Organizations often employ a combination of these storage technologies to meet their diverse data management and analysis needs, which can include:

- Data Warehouses: Data warehouses are specialized databases optimized for analytics and reporting. They consolidate data from various sources, provide tools for data transformation and aggregation, and support complex queries for business intelligence (BI) and decision-making.

- Data Lakes: Data lakes are storage repositories that can store vast amounts of raw data in their native format. They accommodate structured, semi-structured, and unstructured data, enabling organizations to perform advanced analytics, machine learning, and data exploration.

- Cloud Data Solutions: Data in the cloud refers to storing, managing, and accessing data over the internet through cloud computing services provided by third-party providers. Instead of storing data on local servers or storage devices, organizations leverage remote servers and infrastructure managed by cloud service providers.

Despite the growing discipline of data storage, many state and local government employees continue (when allowed) to store an inordinate number of files on their local drives, making them largely inaccessible to AI systems. This presents a troubling dilemma for data managers who strive for data access and storage policies. Hence, there is a need for enhanced data governance.

Data Governance

Data governance is the framework of policies, processes, and controls that define how organizations manage and utilize their data assets effectively, responsibly, and securely. It encompasses establishing guidelines, standards, and procedures to ensure that data is managed to align with organizational goals, regulatory requirements, and best practices.

Key components of data governance include:

- Data Quality Management: Ensuring that data is accurate, complete, consistent, and relevant for its intended use. This involves implementing processes for data validation, cleansing, and enrichment to maintain data quality throughout its lifecycle.

- Data Security and Privacy: Protecting data against unauthorized access, manipulation, and breaches. This includes implementing access controls, encryption, and data masking techniques to safeguard sensitive information and comply with privacy regulations such as GDPR, HIPAA, or CCPA.

- Data Stewardship: Assigning ownership and accountability for data assets to individuals or teams within the organization. Data stewards are responsible for defining data standards, resolving issues, and ensuring compliance with data governance policies.

- Data Lifecycle Management: Systematic data management from creation to retirement. This involves defining processes for data capture, storage, archival, and disposal and establishing retention policies based on legal, regulatory, and business requirements.

- Metadata Management: Capturing and maintaining metadata, which provides context and descriptive information about data assets. This includes metadata such as data lineage, dictionaries, and data classifications, facilitating data discovery, understanding, and governance.

- Data Access and Usage Policies: Establishing guidelines for accessing and using data to ensure it is used appropriately and ethically. This includes defining user roles and permissions, data access controls, and audit trails to track data usage and enforce compliance.

- Compliance and Regulatory Alignment: Ensuring data governance practices comply with relevant laws, regulations, and industry standards. This may involve conducting regular audits, assessments, and risk management activities to identify and mitigate compliance risks.

- Data Governance Council or Committee: Establishing a governance body responsible for overseeing and governing data management activities. This council typically includes representatives from different business units and IT, legal, and compliance functions to provide guidance and decision-making authority.

- Chief Data Officer: With or without a data governance council or committee, the primary role of a Chief Data Officer (CDO) is to oversee the management, governance, and utilization of an organization's data assets to drive business value, innovation, and competitive advantage. The CDO is responsible for developing and executing a comprehensive data strategy aligned with the organization's goals and objectives.

Overall, effective data governance helps organizations maximize the value of their data assets, mitigate risks, ensure compliance, and build trust with stakeholders by demonstrating responsible and ethical data management practices.

Most attention is focused on open AI systems. Open AI systems, like ChatGPT, draw from all sources of data well outside of any government, business, or organization. By comparison, a closed AI system draws upon data that is limited to the data it can access, such as sensitive government records, etc. Understanding the advantages and disadvantages can help one better appreciate which form can work best given a governmental entity's strategic objectives.

Open vs. Closed AI Systems

By its very name, open AI is an open and "free" application that has been so busy at times it has had to turn people away or ask them to return later. Some have complained that this has occurred (though far less often) on paid subscriptions too. An OpenAI system typically refers to any software or artificial intelligence technology developed by companies like OpenAI and Google, an organization focused on advancing artificial intelligence in a safe and ethical manner. OpenAI's systems are designed to solve various tasks, ranging from natural language understanding and generation to computer vision, reinforcement learning, and more. These systems are often built using advanced machine learning techniques, including deep learning neural networks.

Of course, the most well-known OpenAI system is the GPT (Generative Pre-trained Transformer) series, which includes models like GPT-3 and GPT-4. These models are designed for natural language processing tasks, such as text generation, summarization, translation, question answering, and more. They are trained on substantial amounts of text data from the Internet and can generate human-like text based on the input provided to them.

Another notable OpenAI system is DALL-E, a neural network-based model capable of generating images from textual descriptions. Based on the input it receives, DALL-E can create unique and creative images, demonstrating the potential for AI to be used in creative fields like art and design.

It should be pointed out that there are a handful of other open generative AI systems, such as Perplexity AI and Google's Gemini. Some relatively smaller companies utilize the larger platforms and then customize them to their own needs, applications, and clients. You can imagine the magnitude and expense of computer processing and storage, limiting the number of individual companies in this competitive field.

The Public Domain

So, what happens when a document is fed into a generative AI system? Does it become public domain? The answer is it is not supposed to. Documents or text inputs that are provided to ChatGPT or any similar AI model do not become public unless the user explicitly chooses to share them. When a document is downloaded into ChatGPT or any AI system, it is processed internally by the model to generate responses or perform tasks requested by the user. The document's content remains private and is not shared with anyone outside the AI system.

However, it is important to note that it's essential to be cautious about sharing sensitive or confidential information with AI systems, as there is always a risk of inadvertent data exposure or privacy breaches. Users should carefully review the privacy policies and terms of service of the AI platform they are using to understand how their data is handled and protected. Users should exercise discretion when sharing sensitive information with AI models or any online service.

Closed AI Systems

A Closed AI system refers to an artificial intelligence system that operates within a limited environment or under restricted access conditions. Unlike OpenAI systems, which are developed with principles of openness, collaboration, and transparency, Closed AI systems are typically proprietary and may have limited availability to the public or specific user groups. This may particularly attract state and local governments requiring data to remain in a closed and protected environment. This is especially true when analyzing sensitive documents and or data.

Here are some characteristics of Closed AI systems:

- Access: Closed AI systems are often developed by organizations for internal use or specific clients. Access to these systems may be restricted to authorized personnel or customers who have been granted permission or licenses to use the technology.

- Proprietary Technology: The underlying algorithms, models, and datasets used in Closed AI systems are usually proprietary and owned by the organization or company that developed them. These systems may not be openly shared or accessible to the broader research community.

- Controlled Environment: Closed AI systems are designed to operate within predefined parameters or environments. They may be tailored to solve specific tasks or address particular challenges within a controlled setting, such as industrial automation, financial analysis, or healthcare diagnostics.

- Customization and Integration: Organizations that deploy Closed AI systems often have the flexibility to customize the technology to suit their specific needs or integrate it into existing workflows and infrastructure. This allows for seamless integration with other systems and processes.

- Security and Confidentiality: Closed AI systems prioritize security and confidentiality to protect sensitive data and proprietary information. Measures such as encryption, access controls, and secure network protocols are implemented to safeguard data privacy and prevent unauthorized access or breaches.

- Limited Transparency: Unlike OpenAI systems, which emphasize transparency and openness in their development and operation, Closed AI systems may have limited transparency regarding their inner workings, training data, or decision-making processes. This lack of transparency can raise concerns about accountability, bias, and ethical implications.

Overall, Closed AI systems serve specific purposes within organizations or industries and are developed to meet their users' unique requirements and objectives. While they may offer advantages in terms of customization, security, and confidentiality, they also raise questions about transparency, accountability, and access to AI technology for broader societal benefit.

Open and Closed AI Systems Comparison

Here's a breakdown of the advantages and disadvantages of both open and closed AI systems:

Advantages of Open AI Systems:

- Collaboration and Innovation: Open AI systems foster collaboration among researchers, developers, and the broader community, leading to accelerated innovation and the sharing of knowledge and resources.

- Transparency: Open AI systems typically prioritize transparency by sharing their algorithms, models, and training data, which enhances trust, accountability, and understanding of how the technology works.

- Accessibility: Open AI systems are often accessible to a wider audience, including researchers, startups, and enthusiasts, enabling broader participation in AI research and development.

- Community Contributions: Open AI systems benefit from contributions and feedback from the community, leading to improvements in performance, robustness, and versatility over time.

- Ethical Considerations: Open AI systems encourage discussions and collaborations on ethical and responsible AI practices, promoting awareness and accountability for potential biases, fairness, and societal impacts.

Disadvantages of Open AI Systems:

- Risk of Misuse: Open AI systems may be vulnerable to misuse or exploitation for malicious purposes, such as generating fake content, spreading misinformation, or conducting harmful activities.

- Concerns: Open AI systems may raise privacy concerns due to their potential access to sensitive or personal data, especially if they are not properly anonymized or protected.

- Quality Control: Open AI systems may vary in quality and reliability, as contributions from the community may vary in expertise, accuracy, and adherence to ethical standards.

- Intellectual Property Issues: Open AI systems may encounter challenges related to intellectual property rights, licensing agreements, and conflicts over ownership and attribution of contributions.

- Resource Constraints: Open AI systems may face resource constraints, such as limited funding, infrastructure, and expertise, which can impact their sustainability and long-term viability.

Advantages of Closed AI Systems:

- Customization and Control: Closed AI systems offer greater flexibility for customization and control, allowing organizations to tailor the technology to their specific needs, objectives, and environments.

- Security and Confidentiality: Closed AI systems prioritize security and confidentiality, protecting sensitive data, proprietary algorithms, and intellectual property from unauthorized access or breaches.

- Quality Assurance: Closed AI systems undergo rigorous testing, validation, and quality assurance processes to ensure reliability, performance, and compliance with industry standards and regulatory requirements.

- Integration with Existing Systems: Closed AI systems can seamlessly integrate with existing workflows, processes, and infrastructure, minimizing disruptions and maximizing efficiency and compatibility.

- Focused Development: Closed AI systems focus on solving specific tasks or addressing challenges within a controlled environment, leading to targeted research, development, and optimization efforts.

Disadvantages of Closed AI Systems:

- Limited Accessibility: Closed AI systems may have restricted access, making them inaccessible to researchers, startups, or other stakeholders who could benefit from the technology.

Most governments, depending on their objectives, may want to utilize both types of systems, as both offer advantages and disadvantages.

Finally, one of the greatest concerns in state and local government regarding AI is biased. Governments play a crucial role in protecting against biases in AI data, as biased AI systems can perpetuate discrimination, inequity, and unfair treatment. Here are several ways governments can address and mitigate biases in AI data:

- Regulatory Frameworks: Governments can establish regulations and guidelines that require transparency, fairness, and accountability in AI development and deployment. These regulations may include requirements for auditing AI systems for bias, ensuring diversity in training data, and providing explanations for AI decisions.

- Ethical Standards: Governments can promote the adoption of ethical standards and codes of conduct for AI practitioners and organizations. These standards should emphasize principles such as fairness, non-discrimination, privacy, and respect for human rights in AI development and deployment.

- Diversity and Inclusion: Governments can encourage diversity and inclusion in AI teams and research communities to ensure that different perspectives and experiences are represented in AI development. This can help mitigate biases that may arise from homogeneous datasets or biased algorithms.

- Data Quality and Bias Detection: Governments can invest in research and development efforts to improve data quality and develop tools for detecting and mitigating biases in AI data. This may include techniques such as data preprocessing, bias detection algorithms, and fairness-aware machine learning methods.

- Education and Awareness: Governments can promote education and awareness initiatives to increase public understanding of AI, biases, and their potential impact on society. This includes providing resources for AI literacy, training programs for AI practitioners, and public awareness campaigns on bias mitigation strategies.

- Data Privacy and Consent: Governments can enact laws and regulations that protect individual privacy rights and require informed consent for the collection, use, and sharing of personal data for AI purposes. This helps prevent the use of sensitive or discriminatory data in AI systems without proper consent or safeguards.

- Algorithmic Impact Assessments: Governments can require organizations to conduct algorithmic impact assessments to evaluate the potential social, ethical, and legal implications of AI systems, including biases and discrimination risks. These assessments can inform decision-making and risk-management strategies for AI deployment.

- Oversight and Accountability: Governments can establish mechanisms for oversight and accountability to ensure compliance with AI regulations and ethical standards. This may include regulatory bodies, independent audits, and mechanisms for reporting and addressing bias-related concerns.

- Collaboration and Partnerships: Governments can collaborate with industry, academia, civil society, and international organizations to develop best practices, share knowledge, and coordinate efforts to address biases in AI data. This multi-stakeholder approach can foster innovation and promote responsible AI development.

By implementing these measures, governments can help protect against biases in AI data and promote the responsible and ethical use of AI technologies for the benefit of society. Data is what powers AI, and this chapter has attempted to provide a healthy foundation regarding what can be done to ensure data quality that is ethical, unbiased, and provides value to government decision-makers.

Chapter 4: Bibliography

https://infiniticube.com/blog/5-key-elements-of-artificial-intelligence/

https://www.meetsoci.com/resources/knowledge/localized-marketing/branches-of-artificial-intelligence/

https://www.revelo.com/blog/components-of-ai

https://jpt.spe.org/twa/the-basic-elements-of-artificial-intelligence-and-recipe-for-a-successful-career-kick-start

https://www.qlik.com/us/augmented-analytics/ai-analytics

https://www.techtarget.com/searchenterpriseai/feature/Attributes-of-open-vs-closed-AI-explained

https://formtek.com/blog/open-ai-vs-closed-ai-whats-the-difference-and-why-does-it-matter/

https://www.wired.com/story/generative-ai-systems-arent-just-open-or-closed-source/

https://www.linkedin.com/pulse/open-vs-closed-ai-systems-understanding-landscape-klaunch-klaunch-g0x5c

https://www.linkedin.com/pulse/closed-ai-vs-open-monika-g

https://www.linkedin.com/pulse/open-ai-advantages-disadvantages-using-app-development

https://www.spaceotechnologies.com/blog/advantages-disadvantages-using-openai-app-development/

https://www.linkedin.com/pulse/open-vs-closed-ai-systems-understanding-landscape-klaunch-klaunch-g0x5c

CHAPTER 5
Citizen Engagement

Artificial intelligence (AI) and other advanced technologies have the potential to revolutionize citizen engagement by making government services more accessible, efficient, and responsive to the needs of any given population. However, it's important to ensure that these technologies are implemented ethically and transparently to maintain trust and credibility among citizens.

According to the latest NASCIO annual survey of state CIOs, Digital Services came up as the number one ranked-choice regarding which business process could most benefit from AI in the next three to five years.

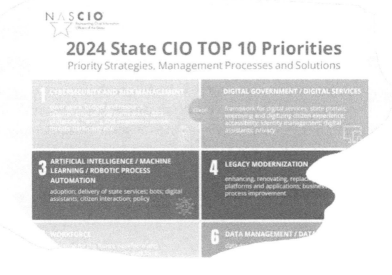

In 2023, PTI conducted the first-ever *AI In Local Government* survey. Similar to the NASCIO survey, citizen engagement ranked number 3 when asked which of the following functions of local government you feel can benefit the most from AI. This finding followed cybersecurity (#1) and data analysis (#2).

Which of the following functions of local government do you feel can benefit the most from AI?
(Table based on average weighting of data collected).

AI can analyze individual data and preferences stored on CRM (Citizen Relationship Management systems) to offer more meaningful responses aimed at better responding to citizen complaints or questions.

These same systems can provide speedy routing of citizen requests to the appropriate officials and, at the same time, maintain a database of all transactions associated with an issue and the responsiveness for the appropriate department. AI-powered citizen engagement systems are not intended to replace mainstream government employees but instead, supplement their work by augmenting staff during peak hours or on nights and weekends when it's more difficult to assign staff.

AI-powered citizen engagement applications, whether through text or voice, can answer basic and routine questions and know when to hand them off to humans, who can then spend more productive time solving citizen issues. enhancing the overall citizen experience.

Based on conversations with state and local government managers dealing with AI and citizen engagement, the following list describes what they see as the advantages of AI applications aimed at improving citizen engagement, services, and communications: Individual needs. This can lead to increased satisfaction and engagement among citizens.

1. Data-driven Decision Making: AI can analyze large volumes of data to identify trends and patterns in citizen behavior and preferences. This information can inform government decision-making processes, ensuring that policies and services are more aligned with the population's needs.

2. Enhanced Accessibility: AI technologies can improve accessibility for citizens with disabilities by providing alternative means of interaction, such as voice recognition and text-to-speech capabilities. This ensures that government services are inclusive and accessible to all citizens.

3. Efficient Service Delivery: Automation and AI-driven processes can streamline government services, reducing bureaucracy and wait times for citizens. For example, automated application processes for permits or licenses can simplify procedures and improve efficiency.

4. Crowdsourcing and Collaboration: AI technologies can facilitate crowdsourcing initiatives and collaborative problem-solving efforts among citizens. Platforms powered by AI can aggregate ideas and feedback from citizens, enabling more inclusive decision-making processes.

5. Predictive Analytics for Planning: AI can be used for predictive analytics to anticipate citizen needs and preferences. This can be particularly useful for urban planning initiatives, transportation systems, and emergency services, ensuring that resources are allocated efficiently.

6. Fraud Detection: AI-driven fraud detection systems and predictive analytics can help governments safeguard their programs and resources, ensuring they are allocated to those who truly need them.

7. Feedback Mechanisms: AI-powered feedback mechanisms can collect and analyze citizen feedback on government services and policies in real time. This enables governments to respond quickly to concerns and adapt their strategies accordingly.

8. Feedback Analysis: AI-driven sentiment analysis can help governments evaluate public sentiment in real-time through surveys and social media discussions, enabling them to understand citizen concerns and improve policy effectiveness.

9. Community Engagement Platforms: AI-driven community engagement platforms can facilitate discussions and collaboration among citizens on various issues, fostering a sense of community and civic participation.

10. Transparency and Accountability: AI technologies can enhance transparency and accountability in government processes by giving citizens access to information and decision-making processes. Blockchain technology, for example, can be used to create transparent and tamper-proof records of government transactions and decisions.

To date, Chatbots have been the most popular application regarding citizen engagement and the growing use of AI. While chatbots have been in use for the past 5 years, it has relied more on machine learning as opposed to AI. Secondly, chatbots were mostly text-based and spoke primarily one language. Deploying chatbots for handling common citizen inquiries can be a practical approach, as they can provide real-time assistance and personalized support, leading to greater citizen satisfaction

The main objective of the earlier chatbots was to supplement staff either after hours or weekends and generally help out during peak demand for services when humans were overwhelmed with requests for information. This was especially helpful during the pandemic. The focus was mostly on determining in advance responses to most often requests for information.

Of course, with the latest in AI technologies, especially with generative AI, the functionality of chatbots is rapidly changing. First, chatbots are now starting to use voice as opposed to text alone. They can be programmed to actually converse with citizens and remarkably, in dozens of foreign languages – including local dialects. The latest systems can actually learn from each customer's experience adapt to different inquiries and know when to hand-off to humans when they reach a certain point. They can add to the knowledge base and, at the same time, provide invaluable data for further analysis and planning. They can spot and report trends and create reports pertaining to every citizen contact, such as type of call, duration, category, frequency of calls per category (issue), location of calls, type of devices, time of day, etc.

While the advantages and benefits are advancing, citizens need to be aware of several key aspects regarding citizen engagement and AI technologies. Without such understanding, all the perceived benefits of AI-powered chatbots could actually lead to mistrust and turmoil. Overall, citizens play a crucial role in shaping the future of citizen engagement and AI technologies.

By staying informed, advocating for transparency and accountability, and actively participating in civic processes, citizens can ensure that AI technologies are used responsibly and effectively to benefit society as a whole.

In order to effectively participate in and understand the implications of these advancements, citizens will need to understand:

1. Understanding AI: Citizens should have a basic understanding of what AI is and how it works. This includes knowledge about machine learning, natural language processing, and other AI techniques commonly used in citizen engagement platforms.

2. Benefits and Risks: Citizens should be aware of both the benefits and risks associated with AI technologies in citizen engagement. While AI can enhance the accessibility, efficiency, and responsiveness of government services, it also raises concerns about privacy, bias, and job displacement.

3. Data Privacy and Security: Citizens should understand how their data is collected, used, and protected in AI-driven citizen engagement platforms. Governments should be transparent about data practices and ensure compliance with relevant privacy regulations to safeguard citizen information.

4. Transparency and Accountability*: Citizens should advocate for transparency and accountability in the development and deployment of AI technologies in citizen engagement. This includes transparency about AI algorithms and decision-making processes, as well as mechanisms for citizens to provide feedback and hold governments accountable for their use of AI.

5. Ethical Consideration: Citizens should consider the ethical implications of AI technologies in citizen engagement, including issues related to bias, fairness, and discrimination. Governments should prioritize ethical considerations in the design and implementation of AI systems to ensure they benefit all citizens equitably.

6. Digital Literacy: Citizens should possess basic digital literacy skills to effectively engage with AI-driven citizen engagement platforms. This includes skills such as navigating online interfaces, understanding data visualization, and critically evaluating information presented by AI systems.

7. Participation and Empowerment: Citizens should view AI technologies as tools for participation and empowerment in civic processes. AI-driven citizen engagement platforms can enable citizens to provide feedback, collaborate on decision-making, and advocate for change more effectively.

8. Continuous Learning and Adaptation: Given the rapid pace of technological advancement, citizens should commit to continuous learning and adaptation regarding AI technologies in citizen engagement. This includes staying informed about new developments, participating in public discussions, and advocating for policies that promote responsible AI use.

9. Improved Communication Channels: AI technologies can enhance communication channels between government entities and citizens. Chatbots and virtual assistants can provide real-time responses to citizen inquiries, improving accessibility and responsiveness.

While some citizens may enjoy the novelty of talking to a *robot* others may find it intimidating. This is where managing expectations plays a significant role. Issuing disclaimers about the use of AI in citizen engagement can be beneficial for transparency, accountability, and building trust between governments and citizens. Here are several reasons why government should consider issuing such disclaimers:

- Informing Citizens: Disclaimers provide citizens with essential information about the use of AI technologies in citizen engagement platforms. This helps citizens understand how AI is being utilized and what implications it may have for their interactions with government services.

- Transparency: Disclaimers demonstrate a commitment to transparency by openly acknowledging the use of AI. Transparency is essential for maintaining trust between governments and citizens, particularly regarding sensitive issues such as data privacy and decision-making processes.

- Managing Expectations: Disclaimers can help manage citizens' expectations regarding the capabilities and limitations of AI technologies. By clearly communicating what AI can and cannot do, governments can prevent misunderstandings and unrealistic expectations among citizens.

- Addressing Concerns: Disclaimers provide governments with an opportunity to address potential concerns or misconceptions that citizens may have about AI. Governments can use disclaimers to reassure citizens about data privacy protections, ethical considerations, and mechanisms for accountability in AI-driven citizen engagement platforms.

- Encouraging Dialogue: Disclaimers can serve as a starting point for dialogue between governments and citizens about using AI in citizen engagement. By openly acknowledging the presence of AI technologies and inviting feedback from citizens, governments can foster a more collaborative and inclusive approach to AI governance.

- Legal and Regulatory Compliance: In some jurisdictions, issuing disclaimers about the use of AI may be required by law or regulation. By complying with legal requirements, governments can avoid potential legal liabilities and ensure that their use of AI is in accordance with applicable regulations.

Overall, issuing disclaimers about using AI in citizen engagement demonstrates a commitment to transparency, accountability, and responsible governance. By providing citizens with clear and accurate information about AI technologies, governments can foster trust, manage expectations, and promote meaningful dialogue on the ethical and social implications of AI in public services.

Whereas state and local governments continue to implement citizen engagement technologies utilizing AI, they must recognize some of the limitations too, Some examples are:

- Data Security and Compliance Concerns: Government agencies face the challenge of managing sensitive citizen data for AI training and operation, which raises concerns about data security and regulatory compliance.

- Ethical Use of AI and Public Trust: The risk of AI systems perpetuating biases necessitates citizens' trust in AI-driven government systems. Establishing transparent practices and involving citizens in AI system design can help build this trust.

- Linguistic and Cultural Diversity: While AI translation tools can improve language accessibility, they may still face challenges in accurately capturing the nuances of different languages and cultures, potentially leading to misinterpretations.

- Algorithmic Impact Assessments: Government agencies need to conduct algorithmic impact assessments when deploying AI systems to ensure that citizen voices are adequately captured and regulatory compliance is maintained.

- Initial Investment and Training: Government agencies often face budget limitations, impacting their capacity to invest in AI infrastructure, training, and maintenance. Starting with smaller, less risky AI initiatives and evaluating their outcomes can provide valuable feedback for future expansions.

- AI systems rely on substantial amounts of data, making them a target for cyber attackers seeking to steal or manipulate sensitive information.

- Ethical and Moral Dilemmas: AI systems can make decisions with significant ethical and moral implications, such as hiring, law enforcement, and surveillance, requiring careful consideration and open discussions to ensure fair and responsible use.

- Many local government agencies lack the resources or expertise to effectively implement and manage AI systems, leading to a skills gap that needs to be addressed through upskilling and partnerships.

- Inappropriate use of AI can lead to a loss of public trust and credibility, especially when used for sensitive public communication or decision-making.

AI technologies clearly have the potential to revolutionize citizen engagement by making government services more accessible, efficient, and responsive to the population's needs. However, it's important to ensure that these technologies are implemented ethically and transparently to maintain trust and credibility among citizens. AI governance is as important as AI technology.

Chapter 5: Bibliography

https://www.nascio.org/wp-content/uploads/2023/09/NASCIO_2023-State-CIO-Survey-A.pdf

https://fusionlp.org/wp-content/uploads/2023/09/PTI-AI-Survey-Results-0923.pdf,

https://www.ics.ai/government-ai-citizen-engagement

https://www.forbes.com/sites/forbestechcouncil/2024/02/02/revolutionizing-governance-ai-driven-citizen-engagement/?sh=58d6e4987fb7

https://www.linkedin.com/pulse/enhancing-citizen-engagement-local-government-virtual-chris-chiancone

https://www.govtech.com/biz/citizen-engagement-tools-build-trust-public-access-to-government

https://www.linkedin.com/pulse/benefits-ai-state-local-government-operations-chris-chiancone

https://www.forbes.com/sites/forbestechcouncil/2024/02/02/revolutionizing-governance-ai-driven-citizen-engagement/?sh=58d6e4987fb7

https://www.ics.ai/government-ai-citizen-engagement

https://www.govtech.com/biz/citizen-engagement-tools-build-trust-public-access-to-government

https://www.ics.ai/government-ai-citizen-engagement

https://cogability.com/top-ai-threats-local-government/

https://www.nlc.org/article/2023/08/31/exploring-ai-applications-in-city-government-the-promise-and-the-risks/

https://www.govpilot.com/blog/ai-in-government

https://www.nga.org/webinars/mitigating-ai-risks-in-state-government/

CHAPTER 6
AI and Cybersecurity

For good or bad (perhaps both) artificial intelligence is quickly changing how we work, how we think, and how we organize. It, therefore, is no surprise how AI is now playing a starring role in cybersecurity. Not that long ago IT staff were assigned to review activity logs that showed practically all electronic transaction flow seeking anomalies and outliers that could possibly indicate cyber intrusions or illegal activity. This task was tedious, boring, and downright slow. Soon, machines would be tasked with doing what humans had once done, albeit much faster, and they would be trained to look for discrepancies based on pre-determined limits. This was an innovation at its best – until AI took hold.

Today AI technologies add new dimensions in protecting both reactively and proactively regarding cybersecurity. Better yet, it self-learns and adjusts accordingly. Some cyber veterans worry about being over-reliant on AI because, until now, nothing beats human intuition. What if AI systems were themselves hacked, infiltrated, and manipulated? But this has not slowed down the allure of AI and cybersecurity.

In 2023, PTI added a new question to its annual City and County Survey, asking, "Are you turning to more vendors that utilize AI solutions for cybersecurity support?" While AI has been around for many years, it appears that interest in AI and cybersecurity has reached renewed and heightened interest; 40% responded with a "yes." One can easily anticipate this number to rise each year moving forward.

Are you turning more to vendors that utilize AI solutions for cybersecurity support?

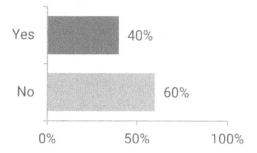

Of course, like all entities of government, much of any pivot to AI cybersecurity tools are wholly dependent on the vendor and managed service provider community offerings. So, when one considers the many challenges of sustainable cybersecurity budgets, staff training, retention, and recruitment - automation becomes increasingly important. Regardless of the noted efficiencies in the use of AI, it still comes with a price and the need for continuous training and, ironically, monitoring. So here we have AI monitoring us, and then we still have a responsibility to monitor AI.

AI certainly holds considerable promise when one considers that AI systems are 24/7; they never sleep, call in sick, or go on vacation; AI is superior at finding patterns and anomalies in milliseconds as opposed to days or weeks. Despite the noted advantages, many local government tech leaders remain uncertain about what is possible or available. So, the timely question of the day is, how can AI assist in cybersecurity operations to protect our cities and counties? Realistically, local governments can utilize AI in cybersecurity to enhance or supplement their ability to protect sensitive data, infrastructure, and systems from cyber threats. So exactly how can AI assist local governments?

Here are several ways – 15 in all - in which AI can be leveraged for cybersecurity in the context of local governments:

1. Threat Detection and Analysis:
   Intrusion Detection: AI can analyze network traffic patterns and detect anomalies indicating unauthorized access or suspicious activities.

2. Behavioral Analytics:
   AI can monitor user and system behavior to identify deviations from normal patterns, helping to detect insider threats and advanced persistent threats (APTs).

3. Malware Detection:
   AI-powered antivirus solutions can recognize and quarantine malware, including new and previously unknown variants.

4. Predictive Analytics:
   AI can analyze historical data to predict future cyber threats and vulnerabilities, allowing local governments to proactively address security weaknesses.

5. Vulnerability Assessment:

AI can automate vulnerability scanning and assessment, identifying weaknesses in software, systems, and configurations that must be patched or updated.

6. Threat Intelligence:

   AI can gather and analyze threat intelligence from various sources to provide local governments real-time information about emerging threats and vulnerabilities.

7. Security Automation and Orchestration:

   AI-driven automation can streamline incident response by automatically containing and mitigating threats, reducing the workload on cybersecurity teams.

8. User and Entity Behavior Analytics (UEBA):

   AI can analyze user and entity behavior to detect anomalies indicating compromised accounts or insider threats.

9. Phishing Detection:

   AI can help identify phishing emails and malicious links, reducing the risk of employees becoming victims of phishing attacks.

10. Security Monitoring and Alerts:

    AI can continuously monitor logs, events, and network traffic to provide real-time alerts and notifications when suspicious activities are detected.

11. Threat Hunting:

    AI can assist in threat hunting by identifying hidden threats within an organization's network and data.

12. Incident Response:

    AI can aid in incident response by providing recommendations on how to contain and mitigate security incidents more effectively.

13. Access Control and Identity Management:

    AI can enhance access control mechanisms by analyzing user behavior and adjusting access privileges accordingly.

14. Compliance Monitoring:
   AI can help local governments ensure compliance with cybersecurity regulations and standards by continuously monitoring and reporting on security posture.

15. Security Awareness Training:
   AI-driven tools can help provide personalized and interactive cybersecurity training to local government employees, improving their ability to recognize and respond to threats.

When AI is compared to traditional cybersecurity tools, the latter's limitations and weaknesses stand out. Here are a few examples of such limitations:

• Complexity and Cost: Traditional solutions are often expensive, difficult to scale, and require extensive resources, leading to poor management and impractical patches and updates.

- Inability to Adapt: Traditional tools lack the agility of cloud-native applications, making them less capable of supporting the speed and scale required in modern business environments.

- Scalability Challenges: Traditional cybersecurity stacks consisting of multiple tools can be extremely complex and challenging to manage, especially as organizations scale. This leads to an elevated level of "noise" and an overwhelming number of alerts that are difficult to manage.

- Limited Threat Detection Capabilities: Traditional methods such as vulnerability assessments and penetration testing may not be able to identify unknown or emerging threats, leading to a narrow view of an organization's cybersecurity risks.

- Manual Data Correlation: Traditional rules-based cybersecurity platforms often require manual data correlation and extraction from multiple sources, leading to partial and disparate data insights.

- Ineffective Network Monitoring in Cloud Environments: In cloud computing environments, traditional network monitoring tools face challenges in determining responsibility for monitoring and protecting specific assets and data and in accessing data and systems.

While it's important for local governments to consider their jurisdiction's specific needs, resources, and regulatory requirements, this becomes more challenging when it comes to AI and cybersecurity.

Experts agree that when considering AI in any application, strong data privacy and ethical considerations must be made to ensure responsible and secure AI implementation.

As local governments battle the likes of cyber-criminals and nation-states, there is a growing concern that AI can also be used *against* the tools governments use in cyber protection. Not only must humans remain actively in charge, but they must also be ready to continuously upgrade their digital infrastructure and seek new tools as weapons against any cyber-attacks. It is easy to foresee the greater sophistication of attacks, let alone their frequency. As has been said many times, local government must get it right all the time – but the bad guys only need to succeed once.

Integrating AI into state and local government cybersecurity comes with several obstacles, including:

- Resource Constraints: Many state and local governments operate with limited budgets and resources. Acquiring and implementing AI technology can be costly, and ongoing maintenance and training require additional resources.

- Legacy Systems: State and local governments often rely on outdated legacy systems that may not be compatible with AI integration. Upgrading or replacing these systems to work with AI can be challenging and expensive.

- Data Privacy and Security Concerns: Government agencies handle sensitive data, and ensuring the privacy and security of this data is paramount. Integrating AI systems requires careful consideration of data privacy laws and security protocols to prevent unauthorized access or breaches.

- Regulatory Compliance: Government agencies must comply with various regulations and standards regarding data protection and cybersecurity. Integrating AI systems may raise compliance concerns that must be addressed to ensure adherence to relevant laws and regulations.

- Skills Gap: Implementing and managing AI systems requires specialized skills and expertise. State and local government IT departments may lack the necessary talent to effectively deploy and maintain AI technology.

- Interoperability: Government agencies must often collaborate and share data across different departments and jurisdictions. Ensuring interoperability between AI systems and existing IT infrastructure is essential for seamless operation and information sharing.

- Ethical and Bias Concerns: AI algorithms can perpetuate biases in the data used to train them. Government agencies must be cautious to avoid deploying AI systems that discriminate against certain groups or individuals.

- Resistance to Change: Resistance to change within government agencies can impede the adoption of innovative technologies like AI. Overcoming bureaucratic inertia and gaining buy-in from stakeholders is crucial for successful implementation.

- Lack of Clear ROI: Demonstrating the return on investment (ROI) of AI integration in cybersecurity can be challenging. Governments may hesitate to invest in AI without unmistakable evidence of its effectiveness in improving cybersecurity posture and reducing costs.

- Vendor Lock-in: Selecting AI vendors and platforms without careful consideration can lead to vendor lock-in, limiting flexibility and potentially increasing costs over time. Governments should prioritize solutions that offer interoperability and avoid becoming dependent on a single vendor.

AI-powered cybersecurity tools differ from traditional cybersecurity tools in several ways, and chief among them is continuous learning and adaptation. AI systems can continuously learn and adapt to new threats, remaining agile and improving their detection and response capabilities. This contrasts traditional rule-based systems, which are often inflexible and struggle to adapt to new cyber threats.

It excels in threat detection by analyzing copious amounts of data from diverse sources and identifying unusual patterns in users' behavior, which could indicate a cyber-attack. When a potential threat is detected, AI-powered systems trigger real-time alerts and notifications to security teams, enabling prompt and effective responses.

Regarding scalability and automation, AI-powered cybersecurity tools can automate routine tasks such as vulnerability scanning, patch management, and incident response, improving operational efficiency and allowing security teams to focus on critical tasks. And as appealing as many of the AI applications used for cybersecurity are, many worry about the potential for over-dependency on automation – AI in particular.

Hopefully, AI adoption in cybersecurity programs and services will be viewed as supplemental and, at the same time, emphasizing the importance of human leadership as being ultimately responsible and in control.

Chapter 6: Bibliography

https://www.americancityandcounty.com/2023/11/14/how-ai-can-assist-cities-and-counties-with-cybersecurity/

https://www.linkedin.com/pulse/benefits-ai-state-local-government-operations-chris-chiancone

https://statetechmagazine.com/article/2022/09/current-landscape-ai-state-and-local-government

https://www.govtech.com/opinion/4-ways-ai-powered-automation-boosts-cyber-resilience

https://www.v7labs.com/blog/ai-in-government

https://www.techmagic.co/blog/ai-in-cybersecurity/

https://www.sophos.com/en-us/cybersecurity-explained/ai-in-cybersecurity

https://www.freecodecamp.org/news/how-to-use-artificial-intelligence-in-cybersecurity/

https://www.govtech.com/opinion/4-ways-ai-powered-automation-boosts-cyber-resilience

https://www.americancityandcounty.com/2023/11/14/how-ai-can-assist-cities-and-counties-with-cybersecurity/

https://www.cloud-awards.com/the-limitations-of-traditional-cybersecurity-solutions/

https://blog.ariacybersecurity.com/blog/the-problem-with-traditional-threat-detection-and-response

https://mixmode.ai/blog/the-limitations-of-rules-based-cybersecurity/

https://www.riskandresiliencehub.com/challenges-to-traditional-methods-of-cybersecurity-information-gathering/

https://www.techmagic.co/blog/ai-in-cybersecurity/

CHAPTER 7
Education and Training (Humans)

Making Government AI-Ready Begins with an AI-Ready Workforce

There has been much talk about having an AI-ready workforce, yet there seems to be more focus on the need than on how we can achieve this. We also know that AI is dramatically different from any other form of technology that has emerged since the advent of the open Internet. Given AI's speed of transactions, complexity, and potential for mistakes and bias, this nascent technology cannot be entirely left in the domain of science and technology. The National Academy of Public Administration identified "Make Government AI Ready" as one of its Grand Challenges in 2019. In addressing AI Ready Government, we recognize that government functionality still depends on humans and human systems. This means we must identify the main characteristics of an AI-ready workforce.

A broad definition of an AI-ready workforce might refer to a group of individuals who possess the necessary skills, knowledge, and mindset to effectively collaborate with and leverage artificial intelligence (AI) technologies in their work environments. To achieve an AI-ready workforce for current staff, we need to develop required AI training and development that could range from a simple online course to a more comprehensive certification program.

We must also look at how schools of higher learning are adapting their curricula to include these newer skill sets aimed at addressing government needs. Changing or modifying the highly entrenched college curriculum is itself a monumental challenge. Teaching AI in college should provide students with a comprehensive understanding of artificial intelligence concepts, methodologies, and applications while equipping them with practical skills to work with AI technologies. Ideally, this should be infused throughout existing curriculums and at all levels. Given the rapidly evolving nature of AI, the curriculum should be adaptable and updated regularly to incorporate new techniques, technologies, and best practices. Here are some examples of how AI can be taught:

- Multidisciplinary Approach: AI is an interdisciplinary field, and its teaching should reflect that. It should integrate concepts from computer science, mathematics, statistics, engineering, cognitive science, public policy and administration, ethics, and more.

- Fundamental Concepts: Begin with teaching the fundamental concepts of AI, including machine learning, neural networks, natural language processing, robotics, computer vision, and knowledge representation.

- Hands-On Projects: Encourage practical learning through hands-on projects. Students should work on real-world AI problems, implement algorithms, and integrate problem-solving based on real-world problems through existing AI offerings to gain valuable and practical experience.

- AI Ethics and Responsible AI: Emphasize the importance of ethical considerations in AI development. Instruct students about potential biases, fairness, privacy, and accountability issues that can arise with AI applications.

- Industry Collaboration and Internships: Foster partnerships with industry to provide students with opportunities for internships, real-world projects, and exposure to the practical applications of AI in different domains.

- Collaborative Projects: Encourage group projects and team collaboration, as AI development often involves interdisciplinary teamwork.

- Guest Lectures and Seminars: Invite AI experts from academia and industry to deliver guest lectures and seminars, giving students insights into innovative research and industry trends.

- Research Opportunities: Provide avenues for students interested in AI research to engage in research projects and contribute to the advancement of AI knowledge.

- Practical Applications: To showcase AI's potential impact and demonstrate real-world applications across various domains, such as healthcare, finance, autonomous vehicles, and customer service.

- Explainable AI: Instruct students about the importance of explainable AI methods to promote transparency and trust in AI systems.

- AI and Society: Discuss the broader societal implications of AI, including its impact on the job market, privacy concerns, and potential for social good.

By incorporating these elements into the existing curriculum, colleges can provide students with a well-rounded education in AI that prepares them to contribute meaningfully to the field and adapt to the ever-changing landscape of AI technologies. This means courses in policy, public administration, the humanities, and organizational development are a few disciplines that should easily absorb and embrace AI.

In addition to infusing AI technologies into existing curriculums, colleges might consider interdisciplinary courses, programs, and degrees. An interdisciplinary approach acknowledges that AI often bridges different domains and an AI-ready workforce benefits from having diverse expertise and understanding across multiple disciplines.

Beyond those employees who are specifically trained or credentialed in AI, the rest of an AI-Ready Workforce, must be skilled to operate in an AI-augmented environment. These skills might include the following:

- Digital Literacy: Employees should have a solid understanding of digital technologies and be comfortable using digital tools. This includes basic computer skills, familiarity with software applications, and an ability to adapt to modern technologies quickly.

- Data Literacy: AI relies heavily on data, so an AI-ready workforce should be data literate. This means understanding how to gather, interpret, analyze, and draw insights from data.

- Continuous Learning: AI technology is rapidly evolving, and an AI-ready workforce must be committed to ongoing learning and skill development to keep up with the latest advancements.

- Problem-Solving Skills: AI can be applied to various complex problems, but it's essential for employees to have strong problem-solving abilities to identify the right issues to address and to interpret AI-generated insights effectively.

- Critical Thinking: With AI-generated outputs, it's crucial for the workforce to have critical thinking skills to assess the reliability and accuracy of AI results and avoid blind reliance on AI-generated decisions.

- Creativity: While AI can handle repetitive tasks, creativity remains a human skill that complements AI. Employees should be encouraged to think creatively and explore innovative solutions.

- Ethics and Responsible AI Use: AI can raise ethical concerns, such as privacy, bias, and fairness. An AI-ready workforce should be aware of these issues and apply AI responsibly in their decision-making.

- Collaboration and Communication: AI projects often involve cross-functional teams, which require effective communication and collaboration skills to work efficiently.

- Adaptability: AI implementation may lead to changes in workflows and processes. An AI-ready workforce should be adaptable to embrace and integrate these changes.

- Resilience to AI Disruption: AI can automate certain tasks, leading to job changes. An AI-ready workforce should demonstrate resilience to adapt to these shifts in the job landscape.

In creating an AI-ready workforce, organizations will need to invest in training and upskilling initiatives, promote a culture of continuous learning, and foster an environment that encourages experimentation and collaboration with AI technologies. Keep in mind that the field of AI is continually evolving, so the characteristics of an AI-ready workforce will continue to evolve as well.

Note: *The above section was adapted with permission from a that appeared in the National Academy of Public Administration's Management Matters that appeared the week of August 7, 2023.*

Making State and Local Government AI-Ready – Training for Today and the Future

At the state and local government levels, training becomes both necessary and strategic, as few schools currently provide it. Perhaps one of the newly created chief AI officers will be to seek out and provide training for state and local government employees.

There has been much talk about having an AI-ready workforce, yet there seems to be more focus on the need than on how this can be achieved. We also know that AI is dramatically different from any other form of technology that has emerged since the advent of the open Internet. Given AI's speed of transactions, complexity, and potential for mistakes and bias, this nascent technology cannot be left entirely in the domain of science and technology.

A broad definition of an AI-ready workforce might refer to a group of individuals who possess the necessary skills, knowledge, and mindset to effectively collaborate with and leverage artificial intelligence (AI) technologies in their work environments.

So, what might an AI training program look like for local government staff? The following course outline was developed over the last several months as part of conversations with IT leaders and technology practitioners and after a thorough review of the state and local government landscape.

In other words, what are agencies doing now, what can be improved, and what is missing regarding the AI training and educational needs in city and county government?

Many training programs have focused on what not to do, including highlighting the inherent dangers of AI. The most often emphasized areas include privacy, security, bias, misinformation, wrong or misleading information, and copyright infringement. While there are certainly many dangers for concern, education programs need to help guide public managers on how they can use it to solve problems, help make decisions based on data, and form research questions for analysis.

Late last year, PTI conducted the first AI Survey for Cities and Counties, and among its findings, over 90% of responding IT executives stated that they feel they need some type of AI training program for staff- and for themselves. To achieve an AI-ready workforce for current staff, we need to develop required training and development for AI that could range from a simple online required course to a more comprehensive certification program.

Given the rapidly evolving nature of AI, the curriculum should be adaptable and updated regularly to incorporate new techniques, technologies, and best practices. Here is an example of what an AI course might look like, designed specifically to fit the variety of needs of local government. Keep in mind that the details of the course should be customized based on the specific needs, resources, and goals of the local government and its participants:

Course Title: AI for State and Local Government Staff

Module 1: Introduction to AI and its Relevance to Local Governance

- Overview of recent advancements in AI technologies.
- Real-world examples of AI applications in local government services.
- Discussion on the potential benefits and challenges of AI adoption.

Module 2: Basic Concepts of AI

- Intuitive explanation of machine learning and neural networks.
- Hands-on experience with basic AI tools using user-friendly platforms.
- Introduction to natural language processing and computer vision.

Module 3: Data Management and Preparation

- Importance of high-quality and diverse datasets for AI models.
- Data anonymization techniques to protect citizen privacy.
- Practical exercises in data cleaning, augmentation, and validation.

Module 4: AI Tools and Technologies for Local Governance

- Exploration of cloud-based AI services for scalability and accessibility.
- Introduction to AI development frameworks.
- Showcase of AI-powered chatbots and virtual assistants for citizen engagemen.t

Module 5: Use Cases of AI in Local Governance

- In-depth analysis of successful AI projects in local government worldwide.
- Guest speakers from local governments sharing their AI implementation experiences.
- Brainstorming sessions for identifying AI opportunities within participants' communities.

Module 6: Ethical and Legal Considerations

- Case studies on AI bias and fairness in public services.
- Role of government policies and regulations in governing AI adoption.
- Group discussions on ensuring transparency and accountability in AI systems.

Module 7: Implementation and Deployment

- Practical steps in project scoping, budgeting, and resource allocation.
- Collaboration strategies between government departments and external partners.

- Guided exercises in creating AI project roadmaps and timelines.

Module 8: Change Management and Training

- Techniques for effectively communicating AI benefits staff and citizens.
- Addressing misconceptions and fears surrounding AI in local governance.
- Role-play scenarios to practice engaging stakeholders in AI initiatives.

Module 9: Monitoring, Evaluation, and Continuous Improvement

- Key performance indicators (KPIs) for measuring AI project success.
- Real-time analytics tools for tracking AI system performance.
- Strategies for incorporating feedback loops and iterative improvements.

Module 10: Future Trends in AI and Local Governance

- Exploration of AI-driven trends like predictive analytics and automated decision-making.
- Guest lectures by AI experts on innovative technologies relevant to local government.
- Group discussions on the evolving role of local government in an AI-driven world.

Final Project: AI Proposal for Local Government Improvement

- Participants create a comprehensive AI proposal for a specific local government challenge.
- Incorporates technical details, budget estimates, and a comprehensive implementation plan.
- Peer review and feedback sessions to refine the proposals.

Assessment Methods:

- Practical assignments involving hands-on AI tool usage.
- Group presentations on real-world AI case studies.
- Final project evaluation based on proposal quality, feasibility, and innovation.

This course outline includes insights and considerations from real-world developments in AI education and local government initiatives that aim to provide a more practical and relevant learning experience for local government staff.

AI training is something that cannot be left to human resources alone. AI training should be led by – or heavily involved. Further down the road, as AI tools and acceptance of AI as a utility becomes more pervasive in society, training programs will be spread throughout the organization, with the IT agency serving as facilitator, and top management serving as champion.

As stated earlier, the White House issued a sweeping Executive Order on AI in late 2023, which, among many mandates, calls for each federal agency to create a Chief AI Officer. Already, state and local governments are either creating such positions or adding such responsibilities to an existing staff person. There is no doubt that with such a powerful new set of AI-based technologies, tech leadership has once again become more valuable than ever.

Absent any formal training programs, employees should be directed to all AI guidelines and polices that are in place. At the very least outside where in-house expertise is lacking, experts should be brought in from the outside and review the advantages and many dangers inherent with AI in all forms. With Microsoft's new Copilot feature along with Google's Gemini, state and local government employees will need to understand AI's capabilities just like they need to know how to navigate a Word document, Excel spreadsheet, or PowerPoint presentation.

Explainable AI

Explainable AI generally refers to the ability of artificial intelligence systems to provide understandable explanations for their decisions or predictions. It aims to make the decision-making process of AI models transparent and interpretable to humans, particularly in high-stakes domains such as healthcare, finance, and criminal justice. Explainable AI techniques include model visualization, feature importance analysis, rule extraction, and generating natural language explanations, all aimed at increasing trust, accountability, and understanding of AI systems by end-users and stakeholders.

Another way of looking at explainable AI presents a challenge to state and local governments as they attempt to train and educate their various constituencies. Elected leaders, senior public managers, and citizens are seeking answers as to what they can expect from AI and what they should be skeptical about. It might be tempting to merely direct these stakeholders to generative AI and have AI do the explaining – but we know that can never be a substitute for direct human intervention.

Humans are still in charge and thus need to be the ones to do the explaining either through formal training programs or review sessions explaining policies and guidelines for AI use.

Elected Officials

Elected officials need to understand the power of AI and the potential for its misuse. They may be asked to explain how AI is being used in their state or local government to a skeptical public. Overall, elected officials in state and local governments have a critical role to play in shaping the responsible and equitable development of AI technologies within their jurisdictions. By implementing thoughtful policies, regulations, and initiatives, they can harness the benefits of AI while mitigating potential risks and ensuring that AI serves the public interest. Here are six key roles they might undertake:

1. Policy Development: Elected officials are responsible for creating policies that govern the development, deployment, and use of AI technologies within their jurisdictions. This may involve establishing guidelines for data privacy, cybersecurity, algorithmic transparency, and ethical considerations.

2. Regulation: They enact regulations to ensure that AI systems operate in accordance with legal and ethical standards. This might include setting requirements for the testing, safety, and accountability of AI systems, especially in sectors like healthcare, transportation, and criminal justice.

3. Funding and Investment: Elected officials allocate budgets and provide funding for AI research, development, and implementation initiatives within their states or localities. This could involve investing in AI infrastructure, workforce training programs, and innovation hubs to promote AI adoption and economic growth.

4. Stakeholder Engagement: They engage with various stakeholders, including businesses, academia, advocacy groups, and the public, to gather input and address

concerns related to AI technologies. This ensures that policies and regulations reflect the needs and interests of all relevant parties.

5. Collaboration and Partnerships: Elected officials collaborate with other levels of government and international organizations to coordinate efforts and share best practices in AI governance. This is particularly important given the global nature of AI technologies and the need for consistent regulatory frameworks.

6. Education and Awareness: They educate constituents and raise awareness about the opportunities and challenges associated with AI. This involves promoting digital literacy, fostering public dialogue on AI-related issues, and ensuring that communities are informed about the potential impacts of AI on jobs, privacy, and society as a whole.

Citizens

Citizens are hearing a lot about AI, and it can play a crucial role in shaping the governance and deployment of AI technologies at the state and local levels. By actively participating in the policymaking process, contributing their perspectives and expertise, and holding decision-makers accountable, citizens can help ensure that AI serves the public interest and reflects the values and priorities of the communities it impacts. Citizens can play a watchdog role by monitoring the use of AI technologies by government agencies and other entities.

By holding decision-makers accountable for their actions and advocating for transparency and accountability in AI systems, citizens can help prevent misuse or discrimination.

State and local governments may want to educate their constituents just as they do with issues of consumer protection. Educating citizens may be a useful proactive strategy in helping make them more aware of the possibilities of disinformation and misinformation from AI as well as deep fakes generated by AI.

AI and Education

Imagine the controversy some 40 years ago among engineering school faculty who expressed concern that the standard hand-held slide rule might be replaced by sophisticated hand-held calculators. Should this innovative technology be allowed in class during exams? The main concern wasn't against new and promising technology, but instead, their fear centered around how students would lose the connection of thinking through a process as opposed to having it instantly solved for them. Today, there are similar debates and discussions with the advent of generative AI, and particularly the popular ChatGPT. And given the many complexities and allure of generative AI (GAI), the consequences are far more serious. Today, professors are rightfully concerned that students will use this nascent technology to short-cut the learning process and use it to prepare outlines and, in some cases, actual assignments submitted as their own work.

A more mindful review of the pros and cons of GAI in public education reveals some compelling arguments as well as some dangers that must be recognized and addressed.

Advantages of Generative AI in Public Education:

- Human-like Text Responses: GAI produces fluent, textual, and verbal interaction leveraging natural language processing to produce a reasonable continuation of text completion, conversation generation, and language translation from massive data sets of human-written text available across the Internet.

- Personalization and Individual Attention: GAI can learn and develop over time based on an individual's input, interests, responses, or behaviors to provide personalized content, feedback, and performance support to students inside and outside classroom hours.

- Immediate Feedback and Increased Interaction: Students can receive optimized, real-time feedback on their progress and participation as well as monitor their own performance. Conversational agents can provide effective support for student learning, interpreting student questions to provide relevant interactive responses, which can enhance their learning process.

- Adaptive Learning: Advanced integrations can be designed where GAI can adjust instructional methods based on student progress and performance to assess, predict, and optimize student learning with automated learning pathways, sequencing, and pacing of content.

- Accessibility: Improved accessibility of digital materials for students with disabilities by implementing required accommodations, optimally presenting information to increase understanding and support reading comprehension and analyzing patterns from relevant data sources to customize and automate the formatting of accessible materials and support.

- Digital Content Generation: A production tool for students and instructors to rapidly generate presentations, video, images/graphics, text, audio, and video by dissecting examples and learning their patterns, imagery, and distribution.

- Automated and Consistent Assessment: Every student receives the same assessment process with improved accuracy through grading procedures leveraging GAI. For example, identifying features of well-written essays provides more consistent feedback when trained on a data set of human-graded essays, eliminating the potential for educator-based inconsistencies.

- Scalable, Predictive, and Recognition Tool to Complement Human Interaction and Decision Making: Mining past inputs, GAI can generate suggestions, systematically compare responses, recommend follow-up corrections, and augment teacher tasks to provide more time for rich student interaction and enhanced decision-making, thus reducing the strain on human resources.

- Cost-Effective: Over time, the integration of GAI might reduce the costs associated with instructional content synthesis and production, textbooks, supplementary materials, or additional human tutors with pinpointed, personalized, lifelong learning support.

- Informal, Self-Directed Learning: It can be a great supplement to human teachers, aiding in areas where there might be a shortage of human resources, suggesting relevant content, and providing personalized tools to mentor and support self-regulated learners.

Like the slide-rule controversy, it is easy to overlook some of the disadvantages of profound and innovative technology. Its limitations are serious and require recognizing and developing strategies to address them. Here are but a few disadvantages of GAI.

Disadvantages of ChatGPT in Public Education:

- Limited Understanding: Without a true, experiential understanding of learning concepts that may warrant contextually appropriate responses and reliant on statistical patterns found in the training data set, GAI is limited in directly addressing student misconceptions in complex, dynamic problem-solving.

- Lack of Emotional Intelligence: GAI doesn't understand emotions, so it can't provide the emotional support or understanding that a human teacher can.

- Bias in Training Data: Generative models are only as good as the data they were trained on, and the massive data sets used for training these models contain inherent human biases.

- Over-reliance: There's a risk that students might become overly reliant on GAI for answers, discouraging independent research or critical thinking. Students may fail to realize the limitations of what data has been indigested into its systems and thus omit many newer findings that have not yet entered the GAI domain.

- Potential Misinformation: While GAI is trained on vast amounts of data, there's no guarantee it will always provide the right answer. Teachers need to ensure students are still engaging in critical thinking. Just because it looks right and is perfectly formatted doesn't mean it is correct. Those who have used this technology report that GAI systems have made things up which are now called hallucinations.

- Lack of Comprehension, Metacognition, and Self Awareness: GAI lacks comprehension, human-level judgment, awareness, and metacognition of its own output with limitations in its intelligent behavior interpretation of social nuance, self-monitoring, and complex problem-solving.

- Ethical, Security, and Privacy Concerns: Using AI in classrooms could raise concerns about data privacy and security, especially if conversations, interactions, or queries are stored or analyzed.

- Plagiarism: Students may be tempted to over-rely on GAI and submit work without attribution. Currently, GAI systems do not explain where their stored information or responses are coming from. Recently, the US Copyright Office launched an inquiry into copyright infringement in GAI.

- Technical Issues: Reliance on technology always comes with the risk of technical glitches, outages, or other issues.

- Update Limitations: GAI at any given version, has a knowledge cutoff. This means that it may not be aware of the very latest developments in a field, unlike a human educator who can continually update their lesson plans.

Rather than outright banning GAI, public education should develop AI literacy, policies and guidelines, spelling out how this technology can or can't be used. After all, there are many positive and promising applications that can enhance learning outcomes. For example, the nonprofit Khan Academy, well known for its innovative approach to teaching K-12 students, is experimenting with what they call Khanmigo for students, which is designed to provide individual lesson tutoring and Khanmigo Assistant for teachers. It is too early to evaluate its effectiveness, but the very concept appears well thought out and promising. Will tomorrow's students look back with affection regarding their most influential chatbot as opposed to their favorite 3rd grade teacher or college professor?

While we cannot ignore the potential dangers of overreliance on GAI, there are so many promising applications in the realm of public education; their usage should be balanced with human-led instruction, human-centered systems design, augmenting human intelligence, and problem-solving to improve learning and education. At least for today, it's most effective when human judgment is leveraged in conjunction with generative artificial intelligence to empower teachers, students, and future generations to be responsible, creative, and productive in the use of these emerging tools.

Note: This article was co-written by Dr. Alan R. Shark and Dr. Brenda Bannan. Dr. Bannan is a Professor in the Division of Learning Technologies and the Learning Technology Design Research Doctoral Program in the College of Education and Human Development at George Mason University and a Founding Member of the Center for Advancing Human-Machine Partnership (CAHMP). The above section was adopted with permission from an that appeared in the National Academy of Public Administration's Management Matters October, 2023.

Chapter 7: Bibliography

https://www.linkedin.com/pulse/benefits-ai-state-local-government-operations-chris-chiancone

https://www.governing.com/policy/government-policymakers-start-to-take-ai-seriously

https://www.govtech.com/biz/data/how-are-state-and-local-governments-navigating-ai-regulation

https://www.brookings.edu/articles/ai-can-strengthen-u-s-democracy-and-weaken-it/

https://www.cityandstateny.com/policy/2023/10/how-governments-are-approaching-regulation-and-use-ai/391389/

https://www.federaltimes.com/federal-oversight/congress/2023/12/07/democrats-and-republicans-see-role-for-government-in-development-of-ai/

https://napawash.org/standing-panel-blog/generative-ai-in-public-education

CHAPTER 8
AI and the Future Of Everything

Artificial intelligence in all its forms is the most significant technology since the Internet became available to the public. This may well be the first set of technologies that steps out of its own domain, requiring social scientists, teachers of ethics, philosophy, and public managers' attention and participation. It requires public acceptance and understanding. When we look at future trends, there is a tendency to combine AI and robotics; we are beginning to see companies developing desktop companions and AI robotic pets.

More recently, companies are racing to develop humanoids that can conduct verbal communications in multiple languages. Think receptionists, information kiosks, teachers or teacher assistants, waiters, senior home companions, and food servers. With such visions of the future, there is genuine concern for the future of work. Indeed, some magazine headlines have made wild claims such as 47% of all future jobs will be performed by robots. Last year, the World Economic Forum released a report estimating that by 2025, 85 million jobs may be displaced by a shift in labor division between humans and machines.

The *Future of Jobs 2020 Report* was published in 2020 and among its findings are the following:

- By 2025, employers will divide work equally between humans and machines. Roles that leverage human skills will rise in demand. Machines will primarily focus on information and data processing, administrative tasks, and routine manual jobs for white—and blue-collar positions.

Most technologists have tempered their predictions towards a more gradual integration of technology and robotics. In the background, many studies have been published about Repetitive Process Automation (RPA). RPA is a technology that uses software robots, or "bots," to automate repetitive tasks typically performed by humans, such as data entry, transaction processing, and communication between multiple systems. RPA bots mimic human actions within digital systems, interacting with user interfaces to execute tasks without the need for human intervention. Protagonists argue that RPA eliminates boring and repetitive work.

Some advantages of RPA include:

1. Increased Efficiency: RPA bots can perform repetitive tasks faster and with fewer errors than humans, increasing efficiency and productivity.

2. Cost Savings: By automating routine tasks, organizations can reduce labor costs associated with manual work and reallocate resources to more value-added activities.

3. Improved Accuracy: RPA bots execute tasks with an elevated level of accuracy, minimizing errors and ensuring data integrity.

4. Scalability: RPA implementations can easily scale to handle increased workload demands without significant additional resources or infrastructure.

5. Enhanced Compliance: RPA can help ensure regulatory compliance by consistently following predefined rules and procedures, reducing non-compliance risk.

6. Increased Employee Satisfaction: By offloading mundane tasks to RPA bots, employees can focus on more strategic and fulfilling activities, leading to higher job satisfaction and morale.

The last item is often used to justify RPA when it comes to human job displacement – it can lead to more challenging positions thus leading to greater overall satisfaction and possibly higher compensation. However, the economic forces promoting RPA are not the players interested in retaining or reclassifying displaced workers. It is easy to see why workers are concerned. Will they actually have an opportunity for retraining and steady employment?

George Mason University established the Intelligent Automation (IA) Initiative, whose mission is *"to research, educate, and communicate how adopting these emerging technologies can improve public sector organizations' productivity, operations, and service delivery"*. The Initiative will also study and recommend possible governance models and public policy initiatives for IA deployment in the context of the broader economic outlook and the future of work. Of particular interest to this chapter's focus are the results from a survey that asked state and federal agencies what the most common applications for the use of RPA might be.

Across the public sector, a survey report of 167 Federal and State agencies as well as government contractors indicated that the most common applications or use cases for agencies currently using RPA are:

60%	39%	39%	39%	23%
DATA COLLECTION AND PROCESSING	DOCUMENT MANAGEMENT	IDENTITY VERIFICATION	MULTI-SYSTEM WORKFLOW AND ACCESS	CALL CENTER SUPPORT

Source: The Promise of Robotic Process Automation for the Public Sector, A Research Paper from the Robotic Process Automation (RPA) Initiative at the Center for Business Civic Engagement – George Mason University, June 2021.

An updated Pew Research Center survey in January 2024, *AI in Hiring and Evaluating Workers: What Americans Think* shows that many workers who are likely to see more exposure to AI do not necessarily feel their jobs are at risk. In the study, 62% believe artificial intelligence will majorly impact jobholders in the next 20 years, but far fewer think it will greatly affect them personally. Understandably, people are generally wary and uncertain of AI being used in hiring and assessing workers. When it comes to employees being asked about their perception of how AI might affect them, just 28% believe the use of AI will have a major impact on them personally, while roughly half believe there will be no impact on them or that the impact will be minor.

There is no shortage of books, studies, and commentaries on the future of work, AI, and robotics. This issue is not only on the minds of citizens and public managers but is also becoming a growing issue among labor unions. As more AI technologies are implemented, some jobs are clearly more vulnerable than others. On the other hand, AI can clearly make individuals more productive and provide greater insights into their work.

Office automation is not new; however, when you add AI into the equation, the impact becomes greater, given its speed of adoption and enhanced productivity features.

The Future of AI

In 2024 Amazon's Alexa turned nine and continues to evolve in functionality and complexity. It recognizes the primary account holder's voice and is friendlier to that person than anyone else. Apple's Siri is also growing in functionality; both systems can recognize complex voice prompts and usually provide excellent information. Humans have become accustomed to voice commands in our cars, smart TV remotes, and home security systems. It is somewhat ironic that both Amazon and Apple promote their voice assistants as "Smart Speakers" when, in reality, they are also 'smart microphones. Both platforms claim to be smarter as a result of AI. However, for those communicating with generative AI systems such as ChatGPT, Google Gemini, etc., the common keyboard is still the input device of choice for posing questions or seeking to create or edit content. Undoubtedly, we will soon (very soon) be replacing our keyboards for direct voice communications with AI as if 'it' were an intelligent being.

In 2018 Sony introduced its robot dog named AIBO.

Today, it is AI-powered, comes in 4 colors, and operates on version 5.50. You can ship it to Sony's "Dog Hospital" if there is a serious malfunction. It remains expensive, but in 2018 it could not be sold in Illinois. This is because of the state's Biometric Information Privacy Act (BIPA), which regulates biometric data collection, including face scans. AIBO has a camera in its nose and tail that provides situational awareness and can identify family members and determine who's who so it can react to them differently. This is simply an example of policies with unintended consequences. Facial recognition, when teamed with AI, becomes an immensely powerful tool. We know from earlier facial recognition systems that there were biases inherent in the technologies that yielded poor facial recognition amongst people of color and "flagged" and misidentified individuals, causing embarrassment and resentment.

Since its debut, AIBO has continued to grow smarter. It can still be purchased in every state except Illinois.

Facial recognition coupled with AI, has made drones ever more useful in surveillance, public safety, mapping, zoning, site inspections, finding missing people, traffic control, and forest and crop management. Facial recognition capabilities have finally become more accurate and less biased, but more needs to be done and oversight is still important.

Finally, many high-tech companies are racing to develop human-looking robots referred to as humanoids. While AI pets may seem like a novelty, humanoids may help fill some gaps in hard-to-fill jobs. These might include supplemental prison guards, nursing home assistants, teaching assistants, and hazardous waste removal personnel, public safety guards, to name just a few.

AI, Recognition, and Convergence

The future of AI, Recognition, and Convergence holds immense potential for transforming various aspects of our lives. The convergence of Artificial Intelligence (AI) with technologies like big data, robotics, and the Internet of Things (IoT) is reshaping industries and enhancing user experiences across all sectors. This convergence enables enhanced data insights and personalized user experiences, revolutionizes healthcare with improved diagnostics and patient care, and will drive advancements in intelligent transportation with the development of autonomous vehicles.

The fusion of AI with Quantum Computing accelerates computations, boosts AI capabilities, and offers breakthroughs in various sectors like healthcare, finance, defense, and the public sector. Integrating AI into the metaverse propels the evolution of immersive virtual worlds by enabling elaborate virtual environments, lifelike avatars, and natural interactions through AI-driven graphics and intelligent systems. As we move forward, responsible collaboration between policymakers, industry leaders, technology experts, and public sector managers will be crucial in harnessing this convergence's full potential for humanity's benefit.

AI or Machine Consciousness- Implications for Humans?

The future of AI is clouded with possibilities and concerns. In Chapter 2, we mentioned that observers of AI's growth have speculated that AI could reach some form of machine consciousness also referred to as artificial general intelligence (AGI) or even singularity. Keep in mind that neither AGI nor

Singularity exist today as they are still considered in the realm of science fiction. Nevertheless, many observers have expressed concern over whether or not it could become a reality, when and how, and what the consequences could be for humans and their ability to control AI.

To help set the record straight, it may be useful to examine the potential significance of Artificial General Intelligence (AGI) and Singularity and expand upon their brief mention in Chapter 2.

What is Artificial General Intelligence (AGI)?

Artificial general intelligence (AGI) is a field of theoretical AI research that attempts to create software with human-like intelligence and the ability to self-teach. The aim is for the software to perform tasks for which it is not necessarily trained or developed. Current artificial intelligence (AI) technologies all function within pre-determined parameters. For example, AI models trained in image recognition and generation cannot build websites. AGI is a theoretical pursuit to develop AI systems that possess autonomous self-control, a reasonable degree of self-understanding, and the ability to learn new skills. It can solve complex problems in settings and contexts that were not taught at the time of its creation.

What is Singularity?

The term "Singularity" in a technological context refers to another hypothetical point at which technological growth becomes uncontrollable and irreversible, resulting in unforeseeable changes to human civilization. This concept is often associated with the idea that artificial intelligence (AI) will reach a level of development where it surpasses human intelligence, leading to a paradigm shift in how problems are solved, and decisions are made.

There are several key aspects associated with the concept of the Singularity:

- Exponential Growth in Technology: The idea is based on the observation that technological progress, especially in the field of computing, has been accelerating, leading to the possibility of a future where this progress becomes explosively fast.

- Superintelligence: A core part of the Singularity concept is the emergence of superintelligent AI, which would be significantly smarter than the best human brains in practically every field, including scientific creativity, general wisdom, and social skills.

- Transformation of Society: Singularity could lead to profound changes in society, economy, and how humans interact with technology. This could include breakthroughs in science and technology, changes in the nature of work and daily life, and the evolution of new forms of social organization.

- Uncertainty and Debate: There is significant debate among scientists, technologists, and futurists about if, when, and how the Singularity might occur. Some view it as a likely and beneficial event, while others are more skeptical about its feasibility and potential risks.

- Ethical and Existential Risks: The concept also raises important ethical and existential questions about the role of humanity in a post-Singularity world, the risks of uncontrolled AI development, and the moral implications of creating entities that may surpass human intelligence.

AGI and Singularity Compared

Many believe achieving AGI is a **prerequisite** for the singularity to occur. Once an AI can improve its own capabilities, it could theoretically enter a cycle of self-improvement, leading to an intelligence explosion beyond human comprehension. However, it's also possible that a different kind of AI advancement, not necessarily human-level intelligence, could trigger singularity. In essence, AGI is a specific type of AI, while singularity is a broader concept about the potential consequences of advanced AI. Singularity and AGI are closely related concepts, but they are different. Here's the breakdown:

- **AGI (Artificial General Intelligence)** refers to a hypothetical type of AI that possesses human-level intelligence or surpasses it. This means an AGI could learn, reason, solve problems, and adapt to new situations in a way that rivals or exceeds human capabilities across a wide range of tasks.

- **Singularity** is a hypothetical future moment in time when technological progress, particularly in AI, accelerates beyond our ability to control or even understand it. The idea is that AGI, or some other breakthrough, would trigger rapid, self-amplifying technological change.

Being aware of both AGI and singularity is perhaps the best line of defense for technology leaders to get too far ahead of the human capacity to govern it. There is no shortage of science fiction books and movies that feature machines taking over mankind and their self-governability. Today most AI frameworks call for the ability to shut down a system that does not behave as intended.

Concluding Observations

The AI we know today is rapidly advancing, and as of this writing, we are only in the 4th generation. Imagine what versions 9 or 10 might look like. That is why those in government must prepare for further unknowns, build a resilient culture of innovation, and, at the same time, manage change. Now is the time to build foundational frameworks for future thought and action. The vendor community will offer much of what AI can offer, for it is way too expensive to develop "homegrown" varieties of AI. It is up to public managers to purchase wisely and have policies and procedures in place to best evaluate, test, and remain in control.

ChatGPT 10 for example, would likely represent a significant leap forward in conversational AI capabilities, offering more human-like interactions, improved understanding, and greater utility across various domains. However, it would also need to address ongoing ethical, bias, privacy, and accountability challenges to ensure responsible deployment and use. Predicting the specifics of a hypothetical future model like "ChatGPT 10" involves speculation, but based on trends in AI development, here are some potential features and improvements it might have compared to current models:

- Increased Contextual Understanding: ChatGPT 10 could have a deeper understanding of context, generating more coherent and relevant responses across longer conversations. It might better grasp nuances, subtleties, and shifts in topic or tone.

- Enhanced Multimodal Capabilities: It could integrate text with other modalities such as images, audio, or video, enabling more diverse and interactive conversations. This could lead to more engaging and informative interactions, especially in education, entertainment, or customer service.

- Improved Emotional Intelligence: ChatGPT 10 might have better emotional intelligence, recognizing and responding to users' emotions more accurately. It could tailor its responses based on the emotional context of the conversation, fostering deeper connections with users.

- Advanced Commonsense Reasoning: Future iterations could exhibit improved commonsense reasoning abilities, allowing them to better understand and reason about everyday situations, solve complex problems, and provide helpful suggestions or advice.

- Continual Learning and Adaptation: ChatGPT 10 might incorporate continual learning mechanisms, enabling it to adapt and improve over time based on user interaction feedback and training data updates. This would lead to a more dynamic and evolving conversational AI.

- Better Handling of Ambiguity and Uncertainty: It could exhibit improved capabilities in handling ambiguity, uncertainty, and conflicting information, leading to more accurate and reliable responses, especially in situations with incomplete or contradictory input.

- Enhanced Personalization and Customization: Future models may offer more personalized experiences, considering individual preferences, interests, and past interactions to tailor responses and recommendations more effectively.

- Ethical and Bias Mitigation Features: ChatGPT 10 might include built-in mechanisms to mitigate biases, ensure fairness, and promote ethical behavior in its interactions. This could involve transparent decision-making processes and safeguards against harmful or inappropriate content.

- Greater Transparency and Explainability: It could provide more transparency and explainability regarding how it generates responses, enabling users to understand the reasoning behind its suggestions and fostering trust in the system.

- Integration with Real-world Applications: ChatGPT 10 might be more seamlessly integrated into real-world applications and systems, serving as a versatile AI assistant across various domains, from healthcare and education to business and entertainment.

Here are a few additional observations:

1. AI use, guidelines, policies, and governance are essential.

2. AI systems will cost a premium, and we will be asked to pay more to enjoy their full benefits. Generative AI systems are extremely expensive to maintain.

3. We will soon be conversing with AI systems using our own voice instead of a keyboard.

4. Training in AI use will become essential for all state and local government employees. AI certifications may be required for those working on the most sensitive applications.

5. Purchasing AI applications, products, and services requires thorough testing, evaluation, and knowledge.

6. AI outputs must always be checked for accuracy and unintended bias. It is conceivable we will deploy separate AI systems to check on other AI systems to help achieve quality control.

7. Data management and governance will need to be strengthened, perhaps requiring how we collect and tag current and future data.

8. Both Open AI and Closed generative AI systems will be embraced and better appreciated for the strengths and weaknesses of each.

9. Most of us will never be ready to replace airline pilots with AI robots.

"I don't know about you, but I would feel better flying Legacy Air!"

Chapter 8: Bibliography

https://www.weforum.org/press/2020/10/recession-and-automation-changes-our-future-of-work-but-there-are-jobs-coming-report-says-52c5162fce/

https://ia.schar.gmu.edu/wp-content/uploads/2022/03/The-Promise-of-RPA-For-The-Public-Sector.pdf

https://www.pewresearch.org/internet/2023/06/21/as-ai-spreads-experts-predict-the-best-and-worst-changes-in-digital-life-by-2035/

https://www.pewresearch.org/internet/2023/04/20/ai-in-hiring-and-evaluating-workers-what-americans-think/

https://www.cnet.com/home/security/what-sonys-robot-dog-teaches-us-about-biometric-data-privacy/

https://www.sony.com/electronics/support/articles/00202844

https://www.linkedin.com/pulse/convergence-ai-other-technologies-shaping-future-our-world-sharma

https://www.forbes.com/sites/digital-assets/2024/02/06/the-inside-scoop-why-tech-convergence-is-your-next-big-opportunity/?sh=58dca50812e8

https://www.wolfandco.com/resources/blog/technological-convergence-rise-ai/

https://www.linkedin.com/pulse/convergence-ai-quantum-computing-glimpse-future-maurice-bretzfield-lfp1c

https://www.thedigitalspeaker.com/convergence-ai-metaverse-futurists-perspective/

DIGIAL DESTINATIONS

The following are supplemental sources offered to those who seek more information on me and the government. With new books and reports coming out at a rapid pace, these sources were selected for their perceived lasting currency. Future updates to this book will feature more digital destinations.

AI.GOV

https://ai.gov/ai-use-cases/

Artificial Intelligence (AI) and Public Managers: Key Questions and Recommended Actions

https://www.ctg.albany.edu/publications/CTG_AI_Report/

National Academy of Public Administration, Standing Panel on Technology Leadership

https://napawash.org/working-groups/standing-panels/technology-leadership

IBM Center for the Business of Government

https://www.businessofgovernment.org/

Society for Innovation, Technology and Modernization, Artificial intelligence (AI): what senior leaders in local government should know

https://socitm.net/resource-hub/socitm-research/artificial-intelligence-ai-what-senior-leaders-in-local-government-should-know/

US Government Accountability Office (GAO)

https://www.gao.gov/products/gao-21-519sp

https://www.gao.gov/products/gao-24-105980

The White House

Executive Order on the Safe, Secure, and Trustworthy Development and Use of Artificial Intelligence https://www.whitehouse.gov/briefing-room/presidential-actions/2023/10/30/executive-order-on-the-safe-secure-and-trustworthy-development-and-use-of-artificial-intelligence/

National Institute of Standards and Technology

https://www.nist.gov/artificial-intelligence

DEFINITIONS

The following terms represent a broad spectrum of concepts and technologies within the field of artificial intelligence, providing a foundational understanding of key principles and applications.

AI Augmentation: The use of artificial intelligence technologies to enhance human capabilities, productivity, and decision-making processes rather than replace humans.

AI Ethics: The study of the moral and ethical implications of artificial intelligence technologies, including issues related to fairness, transparency, accountability, privacy, and bias.

AI Explainability: The ability of an artificial intelligence system to provide understandable explanations for its decisions and outputs, particularly important for gaining trust and ensuring transparency in AI systems.

AI Governance: The development and implementation of policies, regulations, and frameworks to ensure responsible and ethical use of artificial intelligence technologies.

AI Regulation: The development and implementation of laws, policies, and guidelines to govern the development, deployment, and use of artificial intelligence technologies to ensure safety, fairness, and ethical considerations.

AI Robustness: The ability of an artificial intelligence system to maintain performance and functionality in the face of changes, uncertainties, or adversarial attacks.

AI Safety: The field of research concerned with ensuring that artificial intelligence systems operate safely and reliably, minimizing the risk of unintended consequences or harmful outcomes.

AIaaS (AI as a Service): The delivery of artificial intelligence services and capabilities via cloud computing platforms, allowing organizations to access AI tools and resources on-demand without the need for significant upfront investments.

Algorithm: The set of rules that determine the actions an AI system takes.

Artificial General Intelligence (AGI):AI that can learn, understand, and solve any human-like problem.

Artificial Intelligence (AI): The simulation of human intelligence processes by machines, especially computer systems. These processes include learning (the acquisition of information and rules for using the information), reasoning (using rules to reach approximate or definite conclusions), and self-correction.

Artificial Narrow Intelligence (ANI): AI designed to solve specific problems within a limited domain.

Autonomous Systems: Systems or machines capable of performing tasks or making decisions without human intervention, often incorporating artificial intelligence and robotics technologies.

Bias in AI: Systematic and unfair prejudices or favoritism present in the data or algorithms used in artificial intelligence systems, leading to discriminatory outcomes.

Computer Vision: The field of artificial intelligence that enables computers to interpret and understand the visual world through the analysis of digital images or videos.

Deep Learning: A subset of machine learning that utilizes neural networks with many layers (hence the term "deep") to learn and extract patterns from large amounts of data.

Edge Computing: The practice of processing data near the source of data generation, rather than relying on a centralized data-processing warehouse or cloud computing.

Explainable AI (XAI): A branch of artificial intelligence that focuses on developing techniques and methods to make AI systems' decisions and outputs understandable and transparent to humans.

Federated Learning: A machine learning approach where the training data remains distributed across multiple devices or servers, and a global model is trained by aggregating local updates from each device or server without exchanging raw data.

Generative Adversarial Networks (GANs): A class of machine learning systems where two neural networks, the generator and the discriminator, are pitted against each other to improve the overall performance of the system in generating realistic data.

Generative AI (GenAI): A system using neural network transformer models for natural language processing tasks.

Machine Learning (ML): A subset of artificial intelligence that focuses on the development of algorithms and statistical models that enable computers to perform tasks without explicit instructions, relying on patterns and inference instead.

Natural Language Processing (NLP): A branch of artificial intelligence that focuses on the interaction between computers and humans through natural language. It enables computers to understand, interpret, and generate human language.

Neural Networks: A computational model inspired by the structure and function of the human brain. It consists of interconnected nodes (neurons) that transmit signals to one another.

Reinforcement Learning: A type of machine learning where an agent learns to make decisions by interacting with an environment. It learns to achieve a goal through trial and error, receiving feedback in the form of rewards or penalties.

Semi-Supervised Learning: A combination of supervised and unsupervised learning, where the model is trained on a small amount of labeled data and a large amount of unlabeled data.

Supervised Learning: A type of machine learning where the model is trained on labeled data, with each input-output pair explicitly provided during training.

Transfer Learning: A machine learning technique where a model trained on one task is repurposed for another related task, often resulting in improved performance with less labeled data.

Unsupervised Learning: A type of machine learning where the model is trained on unlabeled data, and the algorithm learns patterns and structures from the data without explicit guidance.

ABOUT THE AUTHOR(S)

Dr. Alan R. Shark's focus has been on technology leadership, governance, civic engagement, and emerging technologies in the public sector, with a most recent emphasis on artificial intelligence. He has taught technology and public Administration for over 15 years, starting at Rutgers School of Public Affairs and Administration. He is an associate professor at the Schar School of Policy and Government at George Mason University and an affiliate faculty member for GMU's Center for the Advancement of Human-Machine Partnership.

In addition to his teaching and research responsibilities, he has served as executive director of the Public Technology Institute (PTI) since 2004. He is co-chair of the Standing Panel on Technology Leadership for the National Academy of Public Administration (NAPA) and serves on the executive committee for the American Society for Public Administration's (ASPA) Section on Science and Technology in Government.

He frequently writes and provides keynotes about technology and government. He has over ten books, including the second edition of the textbook, Technology & Public Management". He earned a doctorate in public administration from the University of Southern California. He is also the producer and host of the podcast Sharkbytes.Net, which covers technology profiles and leadership.

About the AI Contributors
This book openly and happily acknowledges its four AI contributors, ChatGPT, Perplexity AI, DALL-E, and Google Gemini. Their assistance proved invaluable in providing the latest information and articulation with amazing speed and accuracy. Each AI platform is quite similar and yet offers slightly different approaches. With Perplexity AI it provides citations in its answers to questions. All cartoon illustrations throughout the book were prompted by the author using AI-powered DALL-E

.

Printed in the USA
CPSIA information can be obtained
at www.ICGtesting.com
LVHW022351200624
783629LV00035B/1370